Earth Almanac

The clarity of Ted's focus — his ability to capture, say, the dance of craneflies during a winter warm spell — stops time in its tracks again and again.

— from the foreword by
VERLYN KLINKENBORG

TED WILLIAMS

Edited by Connie Isbell
Illustrations by John Burgoyne

Storey Publishing

The mission of Storey Publishing is to serve our customers by publishing practical information that encourages personal independence in harmony with the environment.

Edited by Deborah Burns
Art direction and book design by Alethea Morrison
Text production by Jennifer Jepson Smith
Indexed by Nancy D. Wood
Cover illustrations by © John Burgoyne and © Martina Flor/ Handsome Frank Ltd.
Author photo courtesy of Ted Williams
Interior illustrations by © John Burgoyne

Storey books are available at special discounts when purchased in bulk for premiums and sales promotions as well as for fund-raising or educational use. Special editions or book excerpts can also be created to specification. For details, please call 800-827-8673, or send an email to sales@storey.com.

Storey Publishing
210 MASS MoCA Way
North Adams, MA 01247
storey.com

Printed in China through World Print
10 9 8 7 6 5 4 3 2 1

Library of Congress Cataloging-in-Publication Data on file

FOR DREW, SAM, MAE, GRIF, AND MACY.

May they live in a better world
and make it a better world.

Contents

Foreword

The particularity of nature knows no end, and it is the admiration of all of us who tend to see the natural world clothed in generalities. I write about nature often, and yet it always feels like a summing-up to me — never close enough to the hair and skin, to the bark and soil. I reserve a special envy for the naturalists and writers who dwell among the particulars, who come back from the field scratched and bloodied with precise knowledge of how things are out there. Thoreau is the great model here. It is vastly easier to grasp his literary achievement than it is to judge the accuracy and the particularity of his observations of the natural world. Most of us know what a metaphor looks like, after all, but not, as he did, the right kind of day for finding arrowheads.

This book, *Earth Almanac,* exemplifies that kind of particularity. In the past five decades, Ted Williams has made a distinguished name for himself as an environmental reporter, someone who can be counted on to take his readers deep into the struggle to preserve a vestige of this planet's natural diversity and integrity. To some writers, environmental reporting is just another beat — a place where organizations, institutions, personalities, politics, and money collide, much as they do in almost any realm of human activity. What underlies Ted's reporting, what gives it its pressing value to us, is his profound engagement with the natural world.

Earth Almanac is a book of pure perception, a work in which the observer's presence has been distilled into nothingness, leaving only the world — the moment — that he has seen. This book is a collection of those moments, grouped by seasons. The movement of time is the current flowing through these brief essays of witnessing. And yet the clarity of Ted's focus — his ability to capture, say, the dance of craneflies during a winter warm spell — stops time in its tracks again and again. What emerges is a vision of how complex time really is in the natural world, how it pools and eddies and spills away from day into day, season into season.

You may come away from *Earth Almanac* feeling that somehow Ted Williams is both ubiquitous and omniscient. What he is, really, is intellectually omnivorous. His range is almost as broad as the range of the snapping turtle — "from the hills of Colorado to the salt marshes of the Atlantic and from Nova Scotia south to Ecuador." He is as happy taking us into the intimacies of insect life — the mating strategy of the male dragonfly, for instance — as he is explaining the inexplicable Gila monster. And though the native country of this book is the woods of the northeastern United States — or perhaps it just seems that way because that's where I live — Ted Williams is a native wherever nature is, and that, of course, is nearly everywhere.

The cardinal virtue of most good naturalists is patience. But most naturalists are far more patient with nature than they are with people. One of the most appealing traits of *Earth Almanac* is its unhurried practicality. There is poetry here — a poetry of observation and language. But in each of these brief essays, Ted also makes room for us to stand beside him. He's eager to make sure we know where to look, and he gives us projects to make sure we find what he knows we'll find. His version of nature is one to be shared, to be examined together. "Pick apart some cattail seed heads," he says, and I can feel myself getting out of my chair and walking across the hillside to a spring-fed pond where cattails grow.

VERLYN KLINKENBORG

Preface

"Earth Almanac" — originally titled "Earth Calendar" — is a seasonal natural history column that I have had the great pleasure of writing for *Audubon* magazine, where it was conceived and assigned to me by then editor Roger Cohn. For an investigative environmental reporter who mucks around in political dirt during most every working day there can be no tonic more refreshing than climbing out of the trenches and, for one fleeting week, celebrating the beauty and magic of nature. Writing about experiences afield is a way of reliving them. I get to do it all twice.

I am convinced that these regular retreats into what is pure and clean and right with the world have made me a better environmental reporter because they have reminded me of what's at stake and what I'm fighting for. They also have reminded me that the crusade for healthy, native ecosystems is far from hopeless and that good news abounds. As you read this book, pay careful attention to the many species that have recovered from desperate trouble or that continue to do well or at least hold their own in a world in which the general assumption is that everything has gone to hell. Even now, as I reread the manuscript, I find the good news remarkable and uplifting.

These victories are more than isolated events. They result from new ways of thinking and new ways of responding to wildlife emergencies. Together, they prove that humans can undo the damage they've done and restore the planet. What's more, they indicate that humans can yet prove themselves to be a successful species by living in harmony with their own habitat and with other life-forms. Maybe if we can save gray whales and striped bass, we can save ourselves. I like to think that "Earth Almanac" has helped bring a balance to all my writing, and I hope that it has provided and will continue to provide sustenance to a campaign I've been part of since 1970 and that I now believe will be won.

Like all magazine writers, I am frequently obliged to undertake the painful task of copy cutting, especially when trying to fit my words to the two-page, lavishly illustrated "Earth Almanac" spread. In all cases where deletions were dictated by space limitations, I have restored the original text. Therefore, the essays in this volume contain considerable material that is previously unpublished.

I have done my best to be scientific and precise but at the same time tried to avoid clinical dissection, dryness, and, above all, scientific jargon. Having worked with and for biologists, I understand the risk of anthropomorphizing wildlife, and I have avoided it where possible. But sometimes it is not possible, a fact biologists tend to forget.

Humans and wildlife (particularly our fellow mammals) are not so dissimilar as we like to suppose; we share many characteristics — the urge to play, for example. Biologists have proclaimed that "playfulness" in wild canids, ungulates, bears, cats, mustelids, and rodents is merely practice for serious adult activity, such as battles over territory and social hierarchy. This may be true, but from my observations in the wild, I have no doubt that sometimes playfulness is just *playfulness*. That is, wild animals — like humans — play to have fun.

Consider the essay "Winter Games" in which I report the following: "An otter will pluck a pebble from the bottom of a river or lake, surface with it, drop it, swim under it, catch it on its forehead, flip, and turn back to the surface with the pebble still in place, then start the game anew." Now what useful activity could otters possibly be "practicing" with this game? Swimming agility? I doubt it. They need this exercise about as much as professional baseball players need T-ball sets. Otters, like lots of other creatures, including us, simply enjoy sport. To deny this fact is not only *unscientific*, it diminishes wildlife and the wonder of nature.

I have strenuously avoided anything more than quick references to the human-caused threats faced by the species I write about. From the outset I was convinced that this column wasn't the place for "calls to action." A straight diet of exposés and activism is a prescription for burnout. I wanted the "Earth Almanac" column to be a refuge, not just for myself, but for my readers. I have always seen these essays as a chance to take a breather, chill out, count inventory, and, especially, enjoy.

Winter

The "dead of winter" is an oxymoron. Never is winter "dead"; it only looks that way to those who don't get out into it. Snow is not sterile; it sustains complicated ecosystems from algae that live on its surface, to algae-grazing springtails that burrow up from forest duff by day, to ruffed grouse that roost in it, to chubby-faced meadow voles that scamper through it.

Each time you venture into winter you'll discover something new and improve your looking skills. But if you go out for the express purpose of "viewing" wildlife, you're apt to be disappointed. Wildlife doesn't behave this way. At any season, but especially now, it has a way of presenting itself only when you least expect it and rarely in great quantity.

1

So keep your expectations modest. A realistic goal is one notable sighting per expedition — perhaps not a living thing, but a sign of one: wing marks in the snow and a drop of blood or a feather pile where a raptor has nailed a small mammal or bird; foot and belly tracks of frolicking otters; moose scat where no one thought moose should be, now that they're invading suburbia; regurgitated, bone-filled pellets around a raptor roosting tree; sawdustlike dung and quill bits at the entrance of a porcupine den; deer hair on barbed wire; fox scat perched on stones; the hooting (more like bassoon tooting) of nesting great horned owls, incubating eggs even when temperatures drop below zero and snow piles up on their backs and heads. . . . Get a track guide so you can identify wildlife from their prints.

While many birds have flown south, don't forget that you are south of many birds. Look for redpolls, snow buntings, pine and evening grosbeaks, white-winged crossbills, ravens, red-breasted nuthatches, boreal chickadees, snowy owls, and great gray owls. The harsher the winter, the more likely you are to see them. And while there are fewer birds around now, residents and migrants from the north need more calories and are more likely to come to sunflower seeds, thistle seeds, suet, and cracked corn.

In the Northeast bluebirds and robins are changing their behavior, frequently staying all year. You can keep them around your yard (and give them a head start in the coming nesting season) by putting out mealworms (sold by pet-supply outfits in cloth bags that keep well in refrigerators; don't buy fewer than 5,000 at a time). In regions where there's ice for extended periods, open water will attract birds

as well as, if not better than, food. Drippers (far more entic-
ing to birds than standing water) are available for birdbaths.
If you have a garden pool, keep it clear of ice with a stock-
tank heater. This will have the added benefit of protecting
fish, as well as hibernating frogs and turtles, from oxygen
depletion.

If you dress incorrectly, winter quickly ceases to be fun.
Think first about your feet. Even on the coldest days when
you walk or stand on ice, your feet will never be uncomfort-
able if you wear felt-lined boots. But felt is not great for hik-
ing over open ground; then you'll want to wear heavy wool
socks and boots that aren't laced too tight. Think second
about your hands. I've found that puffy Gortex gloves, more
or less waterproof, work best.

In my humble opinion the only good thing about snow-
mobiles is the suits that were designed for those who ride
around on them. But if you are walking a lot, snowmobile
suits will make you sweat even in subzero temperatures.
So I use the two-piece variety, wearing only the top except
in extreme cold or when I'm not moving much. On days I
wear the pants, I'll remove them and stuff them into a light
backpack if I start to overheat. Your head releases a great
deal of heat, so a wool watch cap that pulls down over your
ears and is easily stuffed into a pocket is a must.

Rousting friends and family from warm living rooms
for "nature walks" will work maybe once. After that there
are all sorts of good excuses to get them next to nature in
winter — cross-country skiing, snowshoeing, sledding, hik-
ing, an impromptu game of hockey or broomball, skating,
ice fishing. . . .

This last pursuit (not with tip-ups but with short, hand-made rods) has provided me with most of my truly memorable winter wildlife sightings. Once an immature bald eagle sculling low through mist when bald eagles were almost nonexistent in southern New Hampshire. An enormous fisher — by far the biggest I have ever seen or heard of — who materialized out of a frozen swamp and, as I restrained my exuberant Brittany pup, swaggered past me, not 30 feet away. I nearly expected him to look up and tell me to get the hell out of his way. A great blue heron who had decided to winter in Yankeeland before this became de rigueur for the species. Often the first red-winged blackbird of the year. Geese and ducks muttering from all compass points, only a few feet away, but unseen in a snow squall as my niece, brother-in-law, and I stood on a long, thin peninsula of ice. Musk turtles barely moving over the surface of the ice and hundreds of feet from open water, dropped there (at least according to my theory) by herring gulls seeking to crack them open as if they were seashells. All sorts of wonderful and beautiful creatures below the ice, viewed through manhole-cover-size holes chopped with a steel chisel: pickerel lying in ambush, crawfish feeding on a dead bass, yellow perch hovering around my handmade "jigger" and powered only with fanning pectoral fins, a painted turtle walking across the mossy bottom, bright dace and shiners, tiny dancing invertebrates.

Once, when I lay on the ice transfixed by such visions, a tip-up fisherman a quarter mile up the lake yelled at me. He was wondering if I was dead.

Bright Strangler

After the last leaves fade or fall, hardwoods across America brighten with bands of scarlet bittersweet berries strung like Christmas lights around their trunks and branches. But that dazzling display rarely brings joy to those who value native ecosystems: The species of bittersweet you're most likely to encounter is an invader from Asia brought to North America as an ornamental in the mid-nineteenth century. Today no habitat is safe from its deadly clutches.

But in the eastern half of our country, save the extreme south, we also have American bittersweet, a much reduced native. If the berries occur just on the tips of the twigs, you've found the native variety. If they grow along the twigs in clusters, that's the alien. Make sure not to spread these berries around.

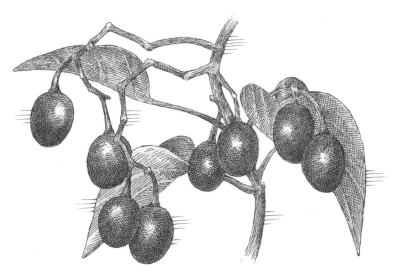

Witches' Butter

Almost anywhere in North America and eastern Europe at this time of year you are likely to encounter a yellow gelatinous substance with the consistency of marmalade. It can even "walk," leaving a slime trail on dry leaves. It is witches' butter. If you find it in someone else's woods, you have nothing to worry about. But if you find it on your property, a witch has hexed you; and to rid yourself of the curse you must pierce and drain her vile leavings with a sharp stick.

Or so proclaim ancient texts. This common jelly fungus, with the even more endearing alternate names of "dog-vomit slime" and "yellow brain fungus," usually appears on dead wood. But it's a parasite, appropriating nutrients from other fungi. Despite its appearance, witches' butter makes a superb base for soups. It has no taste of its own, however, so try to resist the temptation to eat it plain.

Gem of the Winter Woods

America pays little attention to ferns, particularly in winter, when most are brown and withered. But early European settlers had a passion for them, especially Christmas ferns, which remain green all year and which got their name because they were favored for yuletide decorations. None of our evergreen ferns is larger, and none has such deep-green, highly polished fronds.

Christmas ferns abound in the eastern half of our nation, and it's okay to pick or transplant a few. They're an excellent addition to gardens because deer won't eat them. During a thaw, when the snowpack slumps, look for the leathery, lance-shaped fronds lying flat on the ground. As poet-botanist W. N. Clute put it:

No shivering frond that shuns the blast
Sways on its slender chaffy stem;
Full veined and lusty green it stands,
Of all the wintry woods the gem.

Shore-Hugging Whales

Heart-shaped plumes of mist blooming from an early-winter seascape indicate the passage of gray whales plowing south from the Bering and Chukchi Seas to Baja California. Stand on a point or headland anywhere along the Pacific coast and you may spot this primitive, shore-hugging cetacean, one of only three marine mammals ever taken off the federal endangered species list. In this migration, the longest of any mammal on Earth, there will be three to five 10-foot-high plumes every 30 to 50 seconds, then an extended dive.

Frosty Flowers

Long gone are the white, daisylike blossoms of frostweed that provided a feast for butterflies and bees in shade-dappled woodlands and stream-sides across the southeast and south-central United States. But now, with temperatures dipping below 32 degrees Fahrenheit, this tall, hardy perennial blooms again and in the most astonishing and spectacular fashion. When its sap freezes and expands, the stems burst, exuding the intricate and delicate ice formations that give the plant its name as well as the many alternates, including white crownbeard, ice flower, frost beard, frost ribbons, rabbit ice, and ice fingers. It's also known as Indian tobacco because many indigenous tribes smoked its leaves.

Will's Winter Nap

You wouldn't have gotten very far if, on December 28, 1946, you had suggested to Edmund Jaeger that it was time to search for hibernating birds. Like other ornithologists of the period, he'd probably have smiled indulgently and explained that while a few birds — such as red-tailed hawks, white-throated swifts, and hummingbirds — become briefly torpid in cold weather or when food is scarce, none is able to slow its metabolism to the point of true hibernation.

But the next day, as he and two students hiked a narrow canyon in the Chuckwalla Mountains of southern

California, he had an epiphany. There, in a rock crevice, perfectly matching the coarse, gray granite and with its beak toward the desert sky, was what looked to be a dead common poorwill — a diminutive cousin of the whip-poor-will and the nighthawk that haunts dry, brushy areas of the West. Jaeger picked it up, felt its cold feet and eyelids, then placed it back on the crevice — at which point it opened and closed one eye.

For three winters the bird returned to that spot, hibernating through early March. Its heartbeat was barely detectable; its temperature, recorded by Jaeger and other researchers every two weeks, averaged 64.4 degrees Fahrenheit — 42 degrees below normal.

The news stunned the scientific world but not the Hopis. Long ago they had named the poorwill *holchko* — "the sleeping one."

Decking the Desert

Not all of the arid land from western Arizona to Texas and northern Mexico qualifies as "desert," but throughout much of it you will encounter the desert Christmas cactus, a spindly, spiny shrub that grows to about three feet. During most of the year, even in spring when it blooms in yellow-green flowers, it is a thoroughly unimpressive plant. But now its berries shine as scarlet as the tree ornaments for which the plant was named. Here, on this bleak landscape in this drab season, the desert Christmas cactus gladdens the spirit of the lonely wayfarer.

Fishlight

In the "dead" of winter, Pacific Northwest rivers come alive. From Monterey Bay in California to the Pribilof Islands in the Bering Sea, candlefish, a species of smelt, sweep in from the rich Pacific, staging in vast, shimmering shoals at river mouths before they start their short spawning run to low-elevation tributaries. Now all manner of life-forms converge to swill this protein in spectacular orgies — harbor seals, sea lions, cormorants, mergansers, loons, grebes, bears, eagles, beluga whales, and humans. So rich in oil are the fish that settlers used to insert strips of bark in the dried body cavities and burn them as candles.

Native Americans would fill canoes with candlefish, let them ferment for two weeks, then add water, heat it with hot stones, and skim off the clear oil, prized for seasoning and preserving.

Fierce, Playful Predator

Mink watching is a sport you can pursue year-round, but there is no better time than winter, when so many other mammals are dormant or hibernating. From the Canadian tree line south across the entire United States, save the driest portions of our Southwest, these efficient predators are on the move. They fear nothing, including you. A mink may chase a muskrat into its burrow, devour it along with its young, then take over the quarters. Or, perfectly aware of your presence, it may run across your feet in pursuit of newly emerged turtles, frogs, and crayfish.

Confront a mink up close, however, and you may find yourself wearing vile-smelling musk similar to *eau de skunk*. In fact, the name "mink" derives from the Swedish *menk*, meaning "that stinking animal from Finland."

Keep watching and you'll see another side to the mink's personality — playfulness. Like its larger cousin, the otter, it will slide down rocks and slippery banks, or if there's still snow on the ground, it will dive and tunnel.

Treasure from the Winter Woods

Among the treasures to be collected from the winter woods
are pine cones — the reproductive structures of an ancient
genus that preceded flowering plants by 50 million years
and whose Devonian Age contemporaries are now coal.
The cones you'll want to pick up are the larger, seed-bearing
females.

Ponderosa

Sugar

Eastern
White

Loblolly

Hard pines — such as red, lodgepole, shortleaf, long-leaf, slash, ponderosa, pitch, and loblolly — generally produce woody, thick-scaled cones armored with prickers. Soft pines — such as eastern white, western white, sugar pine, whitebark, limber, foxtail, bristlecone, and pinyon — produce softer, smoother, more elongated cones. Even when dry and seedless, the female cones of sugar pines can measure nearly two feet and weigh a pound.

Ripe cones of hard pines make superb bird feeders. Fill all nooks with peanut butter, then roll them in birdseed. Ripe cones of soft pines are best for fire starters. Soak them in melted paraffin or candle wax. For red flames, presoak cones in strontium chloride, then dry; for purple, use potassium chloride; for green, copper sulfate; for orange, calcium chloride (all available at chemical supply houses). For yellow flames, use salty water; for white, Epsom salts.

The Language of Chickadees

Legend has it that on January 6 — Twelfth Night — wild animals can speak. Certainly this is true for chickadees, not that they shut up during the rest of the year. If you learn their language, they'll even tell you what they're doing. Winter is the best time to study them because the garrulous, quarrelsome little birds have the silent woods mostly to themselves. Now they flit about in tight flocks of six or so, hanging upside down from snow-laden boughs and picking insect eggs.

They have at least 15 distinct vocalizations, and each bird has a dominance rank within the flock that does not change, even with injury. "Dee-dee" is uttered after a chase or skirmish. "Chebeche" means "Get away. I outrank you." Members keep in contact with a high-pitched "tseet-tseet." Individuals that have strayed may attempt to relocate their comrades with the familiar "chicka-dee-dee" call. The sweet, clear "Hey, sweetie" song of the male, heard in late winter, indicates the onset of breeding behavior. A bird that spots a predator freezes the flock with a whistled warning in perfect English: "See-see. See-see. . . ."

Color Schemes

When the sun swings low and nights go long, most cold-blooded denizens of the western United States and northern Mexico hibernate or ratchet down their metabolisms. But except in the northern part of this range, the aptly named side-blotched lizard stays active.

Adult males, which measure about six inches from snout to tip of long, thin tail, come in three color morphs. Males with orange throats are bigger and more dominant than males with blue or yellow throats; they defend large territories and harems. But this prevents them from forming strong pair bonds with females the way blue throats do. And while an orange throat can run off a blue throat, the less aggressive blue throat can cooperate with other blue-throated males and thereby run off an orange throat.

Both can run off yellow throats, but females also have yellow throats. So the androgynous yellow-throated males can sneak past the orange throats to mate with their females. But because the blue throats know their mates so well they aren't fooled by the yellow throats.

Professor Barry Sinervo of the University of California at Santa Cruz, who has extensively researched the species, describes the evolutionary scheme as a game of rock, paper, scissors — the orange-throated rock defeats the blue-throated scissors by blunting or breaking; the blue-throated scissors defeats the yellow-throated paper by cutting, but the yellow-throated paper defeats the orange-throated rock by covering.

Snooping on Song Dogs

Winter, when breeding increases their activity and their passage is recorded in fresh snow, is a fine time to snoop into the private lives of coyotes. Coyotes leave straighter trails than domestic dogs, and their prints are less splayed. Side nails of coyotes tend not to register in the print while those of dogs usually do, and coyotes' heel pads are farther from the toes.

If you've seen tracks or even if you haven't, stand at night on the edge of a meadow or lake or any place your voice will carry, and howl. You don't have to get it anywhere near right; the coyotes probably know you're a fake, but often they can't stand not to comment. Soon you'll be left out of the conversation.

In the face of intense human persecution, and perhaps because of it, coyotes have extended their range from the western plains to the rest of the continental United States. Coyotes are larger and more wolflike in the East, where they were first noticed in the early twentieth century. They may have hybridized with wolves on their way from the West or they may have been present all along, mistaken for small wolves by early settlers.

In the West and Midwest coyotes frequently hunt with badgers. A badger will sourly reject a coyote's invitations to romp but will allow it to rest beside it and even touch it, and when the badger approaches a coyote the coyote will wag its tail and roll on its back in delight. The partnership is no anomaly; in fact, when some coyote researchers see a badger in spring or early summer, they instinctively look for its coyote companion.

Solar-Powered Birds

The "beep-beep" you hear in arid country from central California east to Arkansas and south to Mexico issues from automobiles, not those fleet-footed, coyote-eluding cousins of the cuckoo known as roadrunners. Like several other desert birds, this species saves energy by lowering its body temperature at night. But it is almost unique in using the rising sun to jump-start its metabolism. Watch for it on winter mornings — back to the east, tail dropped, speckled feathers lifted to expose a "solar panel" of black skin.

Attractive Repellent

Last summer you may have missed the tiny pink to lavender blossoms of the American beautyberry amid the profusion of wildflowers that brighten coastal plains, swamp edges, and bottomlands from Maryland to Florida and west to Texas and Arkansas. But now the spectacular purple clusters of berries stand out in leafless winter woods. They look unnatural, almost as if they were molded from plastic and belonged on a table in a cheap diner. They're edible, but people who have tried them find them insipid.

Wildlife vehemently disagrees. The berries are relished (especially at this time of year when other foods are scarce) by deer, raccoons, opossums, armadillos, wood rats, foxes, all manner of small rodents, and at least 40 species of birds, most notably bobwhites, mockingbirds, robins, towhees, and brown thrashers. If you find a remaining leaf, crush it and take a whiff. After you recoil from the vile odor, note that the chemicals that repelled you will also repel ticks and mosquitoes, perhaps as effectively as DEET.

Beautyberry is especially easy to grow and will attract birds in fall and winter as well as butterflies in summer. Clean the pulp from seeds by rubbing them with a paper towel, sprinkle them into a pot containing at least two inches of potting soil, then keep them moist. Birds will take care of future plantings.

Desert Jesters

Monkeylike, nosy, noisy, gregarious, playful, busy, inquis-
itive, intelligent, comical. All these adjectives describe the
white-nosed coatimundi, the raccoon's skinny, diurnal
cousin, which before 1900 was rare or nonexistent in the
United States. Probably because of a warming trend, the
species has been expanding its range into riparian areas
and brushy woodlands in the southern parts of Texas, New
Mexico, and Arizona. The coatimundi seems to proclaim
its attitude by carrying its long, ringed tail straight up and
curled at the tip.

Now, in Mexico and our Southwest, coatis are mating
and, though it hardly seems possible, even more active than

usual. Females, which travel in troupes of 5 to 20, admit one dominant male for breeding. At 15 pounds, he is nearly twice their size; but he is submissive. Still, when confronted by a rival male, he'll rear up, puff up, raise his snout, and display his impressive canines in a protracted grimace that can induce laughter in even the most clinical biologists. After the male impregnates the females, they throw him out of the troupe.

Coatis spend hours grooming each other, removing burrs and ticks with their teeth. Like raccoons, they are omnivores, eating anything they stumble on from fruit to small mammals to invertebrates to reptiles to birds and birds' eggs. They communicate by barking, chattering, hissing, spitting, growling, snuffling, scampering, and tail waving.

Jumping Jimmies

They are smaller than chocolate sprinkles, smaller even than coffee grounds. Under a warm January sun or rain they stretch on the snow's sagging surface, especially at the base of trees, as if some mad grocer had slashed pepper bags and danced over woods and meadow. Watch closely, and you will see them leap. They are wingless, harmless snow fleas. Not real fleas, but a species of springtail — an order so successful as not to have changed visibly in 300 million years.

The name "springtail" derives from the appendage under the abdomen, which, when released, can catapult the creature six inches into the air — the equivalent of a human leaping over a four-story building. Unlike most insects, springtails lack compound eyes. They live in leaf litter, bark, and decaying logs in unimaginable numbers — sometimes 100,000 per cubic meter of surface soil.

Snow is not sterile. There is an ecosystem on and in it; and when even muted sunlight strikes it during a winter thaw, the snow fleas scurry up from the forest floor to graze on the algae on its surface. Then, when night falls, they all scurry back.

Fuzzy, Buzzy, and Warm

Honeybees, unleashed on this continent by European settlers, have come to symbolize high sun and high summer, but sometimes you can see them flying in January. When the air temperature edges above 50 degrees Fahrenheit, bees venture outside the hive to defecate (look for their tiny yellow droppings on the snow) and deposit the bodies of their expired comrades. The carcasses mean the colony is healthy, for if it were not, workers would lack the energy for this essential chore.

Even when bitter polar winds plow snow over the hive, there is frenetic activity within. In December the queen starts laying eggs in the brood comb, which is maintained at about 94 degrees by a blanket of vibrating workers, burning the abundant calories of their honey store. Workers feed queen larvae "royal jelly" — a white gelatin they secrete from glands in their heads. Worker and male larvae are fed bee milk — a less nutritious version of royal jelly — for the first three days of life, then bee bread (a concoction of honey and pollen). So much bee milk does a larva consume that its weight increases by a factor of five the day it hatches.

Good Turns

When other Arctic-breeding shorebirds squat on tropical shores, ruddy turnstones patrol beaches on both our coasts. So leisurely is their migration to southern states and Central and South America that they sometimes hang around until after Christmas or even all winter. Watch them as they dash on stumpy legs after retreating waves, flipping over pebbles and snatching the invertebrates that scurry away. The ruddy turnstone dislodges larger stones as if it were a colonial farmer — straining against them with its crowbarlike beak, rolling them over by pushing against them with its breast, and, when a stone is too firmly imbedded, digging out the supporting sand or even enlisting the help of a neighbor. In pursuit of burrowing crustaceans, it may dig a hole larger than itself.

Perched or airborne, few shorebirds are more striking. Wings and back are splashed with white, brown, black, and chestnut red; lots of white shows in flight. The species can be tame to the point of brazenness. Approach slowly, and a bird may continue its investigations within a few feet of your boots.

Catlike Cat Eaters

Throughout our northern states, strange beasts are being sighted in town and country, often in trees. They are dark, almost black, with the face of a cat and the body of an otter. Adult males may be three and a half feet long and weigh 20 pounds, but they look much bigger than they are — the size of a dog or cougar, according to wide-eyed suburbanites.

Fishers, giant weasels that were nearly trapped out of existence in the contiguous states because of their luxuriant fur, are making an impressive comeback throughout their range. They're even colonizing new range to the south and northwest. Fishers are one of the few creatures that regularly prey on porcupines, biting them repeatedly in the face, then flipping them on their backs to expose the quill-less belly. They are also fond of house cats, providing yet another good reason to keep Tabby indoors.

Winter is the best time to find fishers — a.k.a. "fisher cats" — because hardwood foliage no longer obscures your view, and tracks are visible in the snow.

A Plant That Melts Snow

The stench of skunk cabbage is designed to attract, not repel. Pollinators such as carrion flies find it irresistible. In late winter the plant generates sufficient heat — about 72 degrees Fahrenheit — to thaw the ground around it. It does this through an oxygen-consuming metabolism that has inspired one scientist to comment that skunk cabbages behave "more like skunks than cabbages."

In late winter, when crocuses are still underground and red-winged blackbirds hunker below the Mason-Dixon line, look for the purple, streaked hoods of skunk cabbage burning up through an ice-bound swamp. These hoods house a flower that would die without that heat. In April, spring peepers will hide in them. In May, common yellowthroats will nest in them. In high summer, waterlily beetles will graze on the plant's three-foot-long leaves. In autumn, grouse, quail, pheasants, and wood ducks will gorge on the seeds.

Humans eat skunk cabbage, too. Properly cooked, roots and new leaves are delicious; improperly cooked, they will blister your throat. Skunk cabbage has been prescribed for asthma, whooping cough, rheumatism, toothache, hysteria, dropsy, epilepsy, birth control, and the inducement of labor — though not recently.

Winter Bluebirds

Never are eastern bluebirds brighter than when fields and backyards east of the Rockies are draped in snow. The species had been drastically reduced — mostly by starlings and house sparrows, which usurp their nesting cavities. But since the late 1970s, an effort by the North American Bluebird Society to popularize artificial nest boxes has produced spectacular results. As bluebirds surge back, more and more of them are wintering in the North, where they sustain themselves on fruit. During cold snaps they will roost in the boxes, sometimes in groups of a dozen or more.

They eat all sorts of berries, but perhaps their favorite is cultivated winterberry holly. Collect berry-laden branches and push them into the snow. When bluebirds start coming, place some of the berries in a bowl and add mealworms (available in large containers from pet-supply companies; they'll keep for several months in your refrigerator). Bluebirds will learn to take just the mealworms, a much more nutritious winter diet.

Starlings and winter robins will gorge on the mealworms, too, and the robins will drive the bluebirds away, so you will want to buy or make a "selective" feeder. Cut a large rectangle in the top of an old birdcage, then place the bowl of mealworms on the bottom. When bluebirds start coming into the cage, place a board with a 1¾-inch hole over the rectangle. Although that's big enough for starlings, they're extremely reluctant to enter, and the larger hole will prevent bluebirds from getting trapped when ice forms on the edges. Place a twig between the wires three or four inches under the hole so the bluebirds can perch before exiting; otherwise they'll get trapped. In early spring your mealworm-fed bluebirds will have a tremendous head start over all nesting competition.

Dance of the Craneflies

If you would like to believe in fairies again, venture into a woodland clearing late on a windless morning after a warm front has softened the bite of winter. Rising from mossy grottoes by the hundreds, male winter craneflies hover like milkweed silk 5 to 25 feet above the forest floor, their quarter-inch wings and long, spindly legs lit by the muted sun.

Adults of most species are active only in winter, feeding on such sweets as sap, nectar, and fermented fruit. Cure your craving for spring by noting their resemblance to mosquitoes.

Beetle Lessons

If you know children or adults who are squeamish about bugs, there's no better time for treatment than mid-winter and no better medicine than patent-leather bee-tles. There are three species — two in south Texas, one in the mid-Atlantic and southeastern states. Look for these two-inch-long, shiny black insects under dead wood. In the northern part of their range they may be hibernating, protected with glycerin antifreeze they've pumped into their cellular water.

The patent-leather beetle is among the few species in the order Coleoptera that has a social structure, and one of the few insects of any order in which adult males care for young. They communicate with the offspring in squeaks and prepare their food by chewing decaying wood and mixing in salivary secretions that aid digestion.

Although these beetles can eat their way through solid oak, they won't bite. Pick one up and, if it isn't hibernating, it may emit alarm cries that sound like someone chewing on a deflated balloon. After the demonstration there's another teachable moment: Carefully replace the wood you've turned over, thereby preserving an insect-microbe community that may be older than you.

Punctuation in Flight

'Tis the season when even lepidopterists forget about butterfly watching, and that's why finding winter butterflies can be so much fun. Species you'll meet are limited to overwintering anglewings, most notably the question mark, usually brighter than the summer form and named for the silver punctuation mark on each underwing. East of the Rockies (save the extreme northern range, too cold for hibernation and reinvaded by migrating adults each spring) you may

encounter a flying question mark on mild winter days. Check woodpiles and outbuildings, where they briefly emerge from hibernation.

These butterflies rarely feed on flowers, preferring rotten fruit, carrion, dung, and sap. You may be excused if you'd rather not set out the first three of these food sources. Break off a few birch or maple branches and you may find a question mark sipping the sugary flow.

"Who's Awake?"

A twilight stroll almost anywhere in North America, even a city park, may put you in earshot of our most powerful and aggressive owl, the great horned owl. Now, in the cold of winter, they are mating and very noisy. "Who's awake? Me too," is one apt translation of the common vocalization. Great horned owls also whistle, jabber, coo, giggle, and shriek.

Courtship involves all these sounds plus beak rubbing, beak snapping, dancing, shuffling, aerial loops, and mutual head preening. Even in late December the female may already be incubating eggs. Sometimes snow will pile up on top of her, covering everything save her ear tufts and a fierce yellow eye; although the temperature may be 30 degrees below zero, she will stay on her eggs. With this early start, the fledglings will have abundant food in spring, when young animals are active.

Cats Unseen

It's not unusual to spend a lifetime in the woods and never see the secretive, nocturnal bobcat — North America's most common and widespread wildcat, which occurs in each of the 48 contiguous states. But at least you can find its tracks. Don't look in snow deeper than about six inches, because the bobcat, unlike its close relative the Canada lynx, avoids it. A bobcat's track is a larger version of a tabby's — round with four toe pads on each foot and showing no claws.

Bobcats aren't very big; they just sound that way, filling the night with caterwauling so hideous they are commonly assumed to weigh as much as large dogs. But most bobcats are barely twice the size of house cats (with which they occasionally mate, producing strange, stump-tailed hybrids with tufted ears). Follow a bobcat long enough and you might find where it has ambushed a deer, common winter prey. In Massachusetts researchers documented the killing of a 100-pound doe by an 11-pound bobcat kitten.

Feline Flowers

When spring is a promise on the warm wind, look for pussy willows in low, wet places across Canada, south through New England to Maryland, and west to Kentucky, Missouri, and South Dakota. This shrub or small tree was named for the silver, catlike fur on the seeds of its newly opened flowers — which, for the same reason, are also called catkins. If the catkin you are stroking with your thumb has yellow stamens, it's a male, and so is every catkin on the branch because willows are dioecious — that is, only catkins of the same sex appear on a plant.

When you place pussy willow cuttings in a vase, be sure not to add water, because it will permit the flowering that quickly destroys the catkins' fur. Pruning pussy willows encourages vigorous new shoots — a useful bit of information if you get yelled at when cutting them on someone else's land.

Birds on Snowshoes

The ruffed grouse, whose feather pattern makes it appear to be robed in royal ermine, is the most widespread upland game bird in America, residing in all Canadian provinces and 38 states. It is a creature of secret, forgotten places where aspens march into pastures rank with juniper and hawthorn, where multitrunked wolf pines stand guard over stone walls and cellar holes, where bittersweet clutches at the gaunt arms of ancient apple trees and, especially, where snow lies heavy in the winter woods.

As the North Pole tilts from the sun, ruffed grouse grow "snowshoes" from all four toes — protrusions that look and feel like hemlock needles. Frequently a bird allows itself to be buried by the first major snowstorm. Later, it will dive directly into soft snow, where it will spend much of the winter, emerging occasionally to stuff its crop with buds.

Winter Revelers

Cedar waxwings, named for the waxy red substance exuded from shafts of secondary feathers, disperse color and merriment across winterscapes through most of the temperate 48 states. Like carolers seeking wassail, they burst into berry-laden shrubs, gorging on the frozen fruit until it protrudes from their beaks and they have difficulty getting airborne. Sometimes a berry will be passed from beak to beak, down a long row of birds, then back again, until someone finally swallows it. If berries are fermented, the birds may become so intoxicated that they stumble along the ground and you can pick them up and stroke their jaunty crests. The position of this crest expresses every emotion — fear, when flat; comfort, when low; surprise, when erect.

Roving flocks are frequently accompanied by wintering robins and bluebirds and, now and then, a Bohemian waxwing — significantly larger and with cinnamon instead of white on the undertail.

The regeneration of forests and the widespread plantings of fruit-bearing ornamentals have sharply increased cedar waxwing populations, especially in the East. Recently, some birds have developed orange instead of yellow tail bands, a change apparently wrought by pigments in the alien honeysuckle berries they've been eating.

Winter's Bright Bounty

In high country and north country from Newfoundland to Georgia and as far west as the Dakotas, clusters of red-orange berries bow the pliable branches of mountain ash — alternately known as servicetree, roundwood, rowan, mountain sumac, dogberry, quickbeam, winetree, witch-wood, and moose-misse. Feasting on this gaudy fruit are mammals, especially mice, squirrels, and humans, and such birds as pileated woodpeckers, ruffed grouse, ptarmigan, sharp-tailed grouse, blue grouse, jays, thrushes, and wax-wings. Most people find the berries too bitter to eat raw; but with sugar, they render them into wines, pies, and preserves they generally consider delicious.

Twigs and leaves are a favorite browse of moose and white-tailed deer. And where deer populations have irrupted in the absence of natural predators — such as in parts of Pennsylvania and New York — mountain ash has disappeared from the forest mix.

Seedlings are available at most nurseries. They require little winter pruning, but make sure to plant them in full sunlight and in fairly moist soil. In addition to attracting wildlife to your yard and brightening the winter scene, they will ward off the malevolent effects of all witchcraft — at least according to British sources feted as highly credible, though not recently.

Bandit Redoubts

Raccoons, common most everywhere in temperate North America, den in hollow trees, snoozing away cold snaps; but they don't hibernate. By February the polygamous males are out and about even when the temperature drops to zero, visiting dens of females and, most likely, getting thrown out. A female will drive away all suitors save the one she considers her mate (or the one she chooses, if she hasn't bred before). If the mate of a captive female is taken from her, she will cry and pace almost constantly, and if he is then placed in a nearby cage, she will take comfort in reaching through the bars and touching him.

Coon tracks are startlingly humanoid, with toes plainly visible. If there is fresh snow, you can trace the nightly rambles of the males, locating their dens or the dens of females they have tried to visit. Males frequently switch dens. A den inhabited by a male coon one night may be inhabited by a skunk the next.

Pound on every hollow tree you encounter along the trail. Sooner or later obsidian eyes will fix you from behind a black mask.

Mighty Ducks

Long after other wildfowl have fled south — when frozen kelp crunches under your boots and spindrift glazes rocky headlands — our fastest, whitest sea duck finds winter refuge along the Atlantic and Pacific seaboards or on large, open lakes. Oldsquaws (so named because they talk so much and so loudly, but now being called long-tailed ducks by the politically correct) sound like a pack of hounds dancing around a treed bear. In fact, the species' Latin name, *Clangula hyemalis*, means "noisy winter duck."

Now the drakes — with the long, sharp tails — are starting their courtship displays, which include porpoising, head shaking, bill tossing, bill dipping, wing flapping, and neck stretching. Several drakes may circle a hen, gurgling, gabbling, and shouting "ah, ah, ah" or "ow-owly, owly, owly." Oldsquaws can dive to 200 feet, deeper than any other duck, and they fly like hurricane-borne shingles. Hunters who have shot oldsquaws as they veered and twisted directly overhead have found pellet holes in the birds' backs.

Fish Watching

In winter, vast schools of male yellow perch ease into the shallows to wait for the larger females and to gorge on juvenile fish and invertebrates. Watch for them along the margins of ponds or lakes. Or if there's safe ice, chop a hole with an ax, lie on your belly, and use your hands to shade out the sun.

When your eyes adjust to the dim light you'll see the gaudy little fish in the clear water — hovering and picking, pectoral fins fanning, pelvic fins winterberry scarlet, spiny dorsals high and erect. When a female shows up, as many as two dozen males will follow her in a double row, shedding white milt over her eggs, which she deposits in strands that may be eight feet long.

If there are ice fishermen about, wave occasionally to show them you're alive.

Rodent Subways

Beneath the snow there is revelry undreamt of by the two-legged giants who trudge through what they call the "dead of winter." Safe at last from the 24-hour hawk–owl patrol, the chubby-faced, round-eared meadow voles — a.k.a. "field mice" — scamper on stubby legs through a maze of snow tunnels, stopping to greet each other; to preen their long, loose fur; or to feast on roots, bulbs, and grass. In most of the nation, they are the basalt that anchors countless food chains, breeding year-round and pumping out as many as nine young in each 21-day gestation period. Look for their collapsed tunnels when snowpacks slump under sun or rain.

Seal of Good Parenting

In the northern hemisphere's temperate seas, late winter is pupping time for harbor seals — probably the most wide-ranging and abundant of all pinnipeds. The cat-size pup, delivered on land or in water, can swim almost immediately. Sometimes it rides on the spotted back of its big-eyed mother. When it wants attention it slaps the water with its front flippers and, in perfect English, cries "Maaaa." When the mother perceives danger she cradles the pup with her flipper or pushes it beneath the surface. There is virtually no chance that a lone pup on a beach has been abandoned, so don't attempt a rescue.

Six weeks after birth, pups can be seen reclining against the waves, chewing small fish. Before long they will start to catch large ones, holding and rotating them as if they were eating corn on the cob.

Cold-Weather Compensation

Frigid winters have their compensations, among them common redpolls — hardy finches that arrive on Arctic blasts from boreal realms to take up seasonal residence as far south as New Jersey and Iowa. No other northeastern bird has the redpoll's red cap and black chin, and no songbird anywhere has been seen to survive colder temperatures. Maybe its most important adaptation is a croplike structure in which the birds store seeds to sustain them through extended blizzards and long northern nights.

When temperatures drop, stock a feeder or two with thistle or shelled sunflower seeds. But if you find yourself hosting redpolls, don't just watch them from indoors. Their normal winter range is too harsh for most humans, so when these birds visit the United States — often in flocks of 100 or more — you can approach them easily. Note their synchronized movements while rising, perching, and feeding, as if they were being directed by some telepathic drill sergeant.

Frigid Foxes

As tundra slouches from the sun and the aurora borealis dances by day, the only canid to turn color with the seasons dons its luxuriant coat of white or, more frequently in the Aleutian and Pribilof Islands, light gray or steel blue. The diminutive arctic fox, abiding within the Arctic Circle in

North America, Eurasia, Iceland, and Greenland, can deal with temperatures as low as minus 58 degrees Fahrenheit. Small, rounded ears, fur that insulates better than any in the mammal class, and thick hair covering the feet conserve body heat. The arctic fox even carries its own blanket in the form of a bushy tail half the length of its body that it wraps around itself when at rest. Deep golden or orange-yellow irises protect its eyes from the fierce glare of the northern sun.

Now arctic foxes follow polar bears, gorging on their leftovers. At other times they feast on lemmings. Food is often cached, and in warmer months permafrost serves as a refrigerator. Eggshells found in the scat of arctic foxes shortly before the arrival of nesting birds prove they cache eggs for nearly a year.

Fast Food for Eagles

First find a hydroelectric dam, then watch the winter sky.
A bald eagle wheels overhead. Suddenly tail feathers splay,
wings set, legs extend, and the great bird plunges through
swirling mist into the tailrace. It hits the water and rises,
shaking like a spaniel and clutching half a fish in its talons.
The fish was bisected not by the eagle but by the blades of
the generating turbine. Such open-water fishburger provides
a smorgasbord for eagles, especially in regions where ice
limits access to whole fish.

Winter Games

Once they are glutted on fish, frogs, crayfish, or rodents, the
main mission of river otters is sport. In winter they coast
down snowbanks, chattering and whistling at their companions, then bound back up and coast again. They maintain
holes in the ice through which they extract fish, sometimes
with great difficulty because one of their clan, below the
surface, has the other end of the fish in its mouth. An otter
will pluck a pebble from the bottom of a river or lake, surface with it, drop it, swim under it, catch it on its forehead,
flip, and turn back to the surface with the pebble still in
place, then start the game anew.

After years of heavy trapping and habitat loss, river
otters are making a comeback. Look for them in the

Northeast, Northwest, Southwest, upper lake states, and most of Alaska.

Pine-Top Partiers

Little birds with big attitudes, pygmy nuthatches seem to revel in the icy blasts of winter. While other birds are getting out of western North America, you'll hear these noisy sprites flitting about the tops of conifers, especially ponderosa pines, pipping, chipping, chirping, and chattering as they gorge on seeds.

The nuthatch family derives its name from the Eurasian nuthatch, which wedges nuts into tree bark, the better to crack them open with its stout bill. Pygmy nuthatches do the same thing, though on a smaller scale, with pine seeds. In southerly regions and warmer seasons they'll circle tree trunks, gleaning spiders, insects, eggs, and pupae from bark crevices; and they'll come readily to your yard to eat suet and sunflower seeds. They combat severe cold by lowering body temperatures and huddling together in tree cavities, sometimes in groups of 100 or more.

In fact, no record exists of a pygmy nuthatch roosting alone. This sociability extends to the breeding season when, for a large segment of the population, brood rearing becomes a community effort with other birds — usually, but not always, male offspring from previous years — helping parents defend territory and feed young.

Strange Changes

When the sun's passage is still low and brief, and snow lies high like a shaken quilt, male eastern newts begin their prespawning transformation. If their pond has black ice or no ice, you may see them sashaying along the bottom most anywhere in the eastern half of our nation. Now tails grow flat and eel-like; vents swell; hind legs enlarge; and black, horny appendages form on inner thighs and tips of toes.

The most useful words for anyone explaining this salamander's life history are "but sometimes." Usually, larvae transform into a subadult terrestrial stage called red eft, but sometimes they transform directly into the aquatic adult stage. Usually, adults have lungs, but sometimes (when they skip the eft stage) they retain their larval gills. Because newts exude a toxin, fish almost always shun them — in fact, in one experiment, trout died when newts were pushed down their gullets — but sometimes wild brook trout glut themselves on newts.

Winter Butterflies

There is snow in the woods and ice on the ponds, so why are black, purple-and-yellow-trimmed butterflies sailing over the chaff of last year's lawn? How could they have hatched so soon? They didn't; they hibernated as adults in deep crevices and under bark. A month hence, they will feed on nectar and rotten fruit; now they sip sap from the ice-splintered, deer-scraped branches of birch and maple.

Mourning cloaks, as they are aptly called, are among the most widely distributed of all butterflies. You can find them in Eurasia, Mexico, and all of North America, from the wilds of Alaska to the sidewalks of Manhattan. In northern latitudes they also hibernate during summer, reemerging in fall. In spring, look for their dramatic mating dance. A pair will spiral straight up for 60 feet, couple, and probably mate. Then one drops to the ground as if hit by a windshield.

Flash of Red Epaulets

In most of the United States, the first bird of "spring" arrives in late winter: not the American robin but the red-winged blackbird, said probably without exaggeration to occur in every county of our nation. The males — black with scarlet shoulder patches — come first, sometimes in flocks of thousands that blow like coal smoke over the soggy earth, veering suddenly right, left, up, or down as if steered by a common will. Through most of March you can attract them to your yard with cracked corn.

A flock will stake out a large marsh in which each male defends a territory of about a quarter acre. The male does this in a way that gladdens the hearts of winter-weary humans — by riding a bobbing bough or cattail, raising his red epaulets so they flash in the sun, and shouting "Oaklareeeee!"

Weasel Writing

Written plainly in the snow is the personality of this kielbasa-size package of energy. Note — in the rambling trail — how curious he is. Frequent bounds betray his eagerness. Recorded also in the snow are the violent struggles with prey that sometimes outweighs him by a factor of five.

Long-tailed weasels purr when content, squeak when annoyed, and release malodorous musk when enraged or sexually excited. You're apt to encounter them anywhere in the United States. But in the North, where their brown fur turns white in snowtime, you may glimpse only an ebony muzzle — or just tracks.

Frozen Fliers

By aquatic insect standards the life cycles of the roughly 600 species of stoneflies inhabiting North America are normal enough. But one family — the Capniidae, or winter stoneflies — lives in reverse. When frigid weather sends virtually all other flying insects to death, dormancy, or southern latitudes, the nymphs of winter stoneflies crawl from under submerged stones, make their way up stream banks, anchor themselves to rocks with gluelike secretions, pull themselves out of their larval skins, and take to the chilled air as four-winged adults.

Winter stoneflies are no accident of nature; they enter a world virtually devoid of bird and insect predators. Look for them on streamside snow and ice or lumbering along in slow flight like giant gray mosquitoes. Unlike most insect infestations, an infestation of stoneflies — encountered at any season — gladdens those who delight in undefiled habitats. When water-quality surveyors turn up stoneflies in their macroinvertebrate samples, they classify the stream as "good quality" because these insects require clean, well-oxygenated water.

Winter Mushrooms

You don't eat bracket fungi unless you're starving, but what they lack in palatability they make up for in beauty and durability. The semicircular brackets, found all over temperate North America, don't rot away like other mushrooms and usually remain above the snow line because they grow on stumps and trees. Don't feel guilty about taking a few home for decorations; what you are picking is just the spore-producing part of the fungus that has burst through an opening in the tree. Most of the organism is still within — a tangle of enzyme-secreting, wood-dissolving tentacles called the mycelium.

Birch Polypore

Turkey Tail

Thin Mazegill

Tinder Fungus

Watch for two species of mazegill. Thin mazegill is corky, speckled light brown on top and occurs in spectacular clusters, often on willow, yellow birch, and oak. Thick mazegill, found mostly on oaks, has a thicker maze. Then there is tinder fungus, which is shaped like a horse's hoof and good for starting campfires. Birch polypore, the gray mushroom that grows on old birches, was used to sharpen razors. The lovely and aptly named turkey tail, often found in profuse whorls at the ends of logs, has concentric rings of gray, tan, brown, red, and green. Artist's fungus can measure two feet across; use a sharp stick to sketch the best thing you saw on your winter outing on its soft undersurface. When the mushroom dries and hardens on your mantel, the rendering will endure for decades.

Chipper Chaps

The calendar says it's still winter, but when the first chipmunk peeks over the rim of its winter burrow and scampers across your yard, spring can be only a few weeks away. In the eastern half of the country (except for the extreme South), your harbinger will be the eastern chipmunk. In the West it will be one of at least 16 species, all strikingly similar.

The capacity of a chipmunk's cheeks is prodigious. One load, for example, was reported to consist of two heaping tablespoons of corn kernels. It's an easy task for an individual to empty and cache the entire contents of a bird feeder in less than an hour.

While chipmunks remain underground for most of the winter, they don't hibernate. Instead, they sleep for a few days to a week, then snack from their pantries, which double as bedrooms. A burrow also has a bathroom. Chipmunks, the most fastidious of rodents, are obsessive groomers and able to reach every part of their bodies with mouth or paw. Therefore, they have few external parasites.

In the language of eastern chipmunks, a chuck expresses fear or anger; a chip-trill, surprise; a chuck-trill, aggression. When you hear a chipmunk uttering 80 to 180 chips per minute for half an hour, it is saying, "I am a chipmunk, and I am here."

Snowbirds

Dark-eyed juncos — also called "snowbirds" because they waft south from boreal breeding grounds on the teeth of blizzards — are flooding fields, parks, and yards across the contiguous 48 states. The birds you see foraging in your yard are likely "yours" because they usually return to the same winter habitat. In one experiment, nine of a dozen birds banded in a Massachusetts backyard were seen there the following year. If your juncos look different from ones you've encountered elsewhere, there's a good reason for it. There is great regional variation in plumage, with all manner of combinations of white, rust, gray, black, and brown.

Your flock, numbering as many as 30 birds, will form about a half hour before sunrise, feed through the day, then disperse to roost about 45 minutes before sunset. Listen to their seemingly absentminded chips as they forage. And watch them as they raise and flash their tails to show dominance, hop, scrape circles in the snow, and perch like miniature "benders of birches" atop grass stems, riding them to the earth to feast on the seeds.

Winter's Candy

Sapsicles — those shards of frozen sap that hang from broken branches of hardwoods — seem made for consumption by kids and by adults with kids' hearts. If you close your eyes and concentrate, you can taste the coming spring. Sapsicles are sweeter than liquid sap because the sugar has been concentrated by evaporation. Look for them on warm, late-winter days after night temperatures have dipped below freezing.

According to some connoisseurs, black-birch sapsicles have a faint wintergreen flavor; butternut sapsicles are vaguely reminiscent of cider. While red maple and box elder sapsicles are superb, the best are produced by sugar maples, which grow from Canada to northern Georgia to eastern Kansas. Some of these trees are five feet in diameter and may still bear V-shaped scars made by the Native Americans who collected their sap to make sugar.

Fairy Shrimp

In the last days of winter, vernal pools — those pockets of snowmelt and rain that vanish in the heat of summer — teem with life, unseen by those who hasten through their days oblivious to Earth's wonders. Do not be one of them.

You can't be sure you've found a vernal pool unless you identify one of the obligate denizens such as fairy shrimp, an order more ancient than dinosaurs. Keep looking under the dappled surface, between the floating pine needles. First you'll see the two white stripes on the tail; then a translucent creature roughly an inch long will materialize. Fairy shrimp hang and hover, swimming upside down and propelling themselves with 11 sets of legs also used to extract oxygen.

They are there because fish are not. Ducks eat fairy shrimp but also transport their eggs to other vernal pools. There are two kinds of eggs — one for times of plenty and one for low, warm water laden with salts concentrated by evaporation. The first type, laid by unfertilized females, quickly produce clones. The second, actually encysted embryos, result from male-female unions and remain viable through summer dust and winter ice.

Because vernal pools are generally regarded as worthless puddles, many species of fairy shrimp are endangered.

Owls in Winter Sun

On our frozen beaches and marshes, on bitter, wind-blasted prairies, at large metropolitan airports, and in any habitat vaguely reminiscent of tundra, North America's heaviest owl finds winter refuge from the even more brutal cold of its breeding grounds. In normal years the northern tier of our contiguous states is its sunny south. Irruptions are heaviest when the lemming population has crashed in the far north.

Unlike most owls, this one often hunts by day because it raises its young in a land where summer night, if it occurs at all, is fleeting as the blush of wildflowers. Over surrogate tundra south of the Canadian border or real tundra in the high Arctic, the snowy owl floats like the angel of death, swooping down to talon rodents and swallow them head-first. You're apt to spy it while it roosts on the ground — a pair of fierce yellow eyes looking into the sun, then a white, black-flecked body taking form around them.

Scorpio Descending

When the wind is from the south, watch for scorpions overhead as they fly about, propelled by outstretched legs that serve as aerial oars; and when they descend, shun them before noon because morning stings are always fatal. So instructed Pliny the Elder two millennia ago.

Such apocryphal scorpion lore, piling up before and since, is scarcely more astonishing than reality. Some scorpions were the size of crocodiles when, about 400 million years ago, the order exited the sea to take its place among the first earthbound arthropods. Of about 90 species of modern scorpions native to the United States, only four abide east of the Mississippi; and while fatal allergic reactions can be caused by most any venom, only the Arizona bark scorpion can be considered truly lethal to humans, though its sting almost never kills adults.

In late winter scorpions emerge from winter quarters to forage for insects, spiders, centipedes, other scorpions, and small vertebrates. Because scorpions are nocturnal, few people comprehend how abundant they are, especially in our Southwest. Now is the time to set yourself and others straight. Scorpions glow under ultraviolet light, so order an ultraviolet flashlight from any likely source. Like stars reflected on a glassy sea, these ancient arachnids will suddenly fluoresce across the desert floor. But restrain yourself, if you are able, by following this valuable advice offered by the University of Kentucky: "No scorpion should be picked up with bare hands."

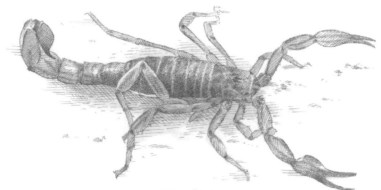

What Groundhogs Do
on February 2

Throughout most of its U.S. range (roughly the eastern half of the nation), it's unlikely any woodchuck stirring on even a cloudless Groundhog Day could cast a shadow. In the South a few of these portly ground squirrels may have emerged from hibernation by February 2, but most are still curled up in subterranean dens that include a bedroom lined with dried grass, a latrine, and an entrance tunnel up to 45 feet long.

A hibernating chuck's body temperature can drop from 99 degrees Fahrenheit to 41 and its aspiration from 2,100 breaths per hour to 60. Yet hibernation does not mean constant sleep. During warm spells the chuck wakes periodically to urinate.

Ice Turtles

For most any American, save residents of the Southwest and far and central West, finding painted turtles basking in the July sun entails no more than a stroll to the nearest wetland. But finding them under or on the ice is a challenge and, therefore, good fun.

Not only are painted turtles the most widely distributed aquatic reptiles in the United States and Canada, they are the most cold tolerant. When pond ice is clear, look for them resting on or moving slowly across the bottom. On warm days in later winter, you may encounter them basking on the edge of retreating ice.

Freshwater turtles are able to hibernate underwater by absorbing oxygen through their skin, but the painted turtle can survive a winter in deoxygenated water. It accomplishes this by anaerobic respiration. Because this strategy produces lactic acid, which disrupts blood chemistry, the painted turtle must break down the acid by releasing carbonate from its shell and bones — basically, consuming its own skeleton. Rarely is there sufficient bone loss to prove fatal.

Next time you see one of these strikingly beautiful turtles, pause for an instant and celebrate the resiliency of nature, and remember that lots of wild animals aren't disappearing.

Woody's Courtship

The pileated — our largest woodpecker, which can knock 14-inch-long chips out of dead and living trees — spends late winter and early spring courting and nest building. Throughout wooded North America, from British Columbia to Nova Scotia and south, you may hear the maniacal, flickerlike laughter of these crow-size, scarlet-crested models for Walter Lantz's Woody Woodpecker. If you hear nothing, pound a hollow tree with a stick and one may come in to defend his territory.

Courting pileateds do much bobbing, head swinging, wing flailing, and crest raising. They will meet on a limb, dance, bow, stretch their long ungainly necks, appear to kiss, then inscribe lazy circles on fluttering, silver-lined wings. Unlike other woodpeckers, they mate for life and each year cut a new nest hole, leaving last year's home for other cavity nesters. The females have been seen transporting their eggs from a split tree to a new site.

Pileated, which means capped, can be pronounced "pile" or "pill." Either way, reports birding authority John Eastman, "will be wrong in whatever field group one happens to join."

Wet Dogs That Don't Shake

Quite regularly in the eastern half of the nation, save the extreme South and Southeast, a fisherman soaking a worm or minnow will haul out a creature "new to science." The fearsome-looking beast, which may approach 20 inches in length, has frog feet, leopard spots, a dog snout, an eel tail, and an otherworldly collar of fleshy red frills. Usually the local wildlife expert identifies it as a mudpuppy, a permanently aquatic salamander with external gills (its lungs are used as a fish's swim bladder is: to regulate buoyancy).

A winter evening is a fine time for mudpuppy watching, especially if the pond ice is walkable and clear. In your flashlight beam you'll see them stalking across the bottom. You may witness their courtship — the male walking around, over, and even under the female as she stands on rigid legs.

Pungent Prowlers

On the first warm evenings of the Hunger Moon, in late February, you will start to see or nose male skunks as they ramble through town and country in search of females. Probably they are striped skunks, the most ubiquitous of North America's four species. Skunks don't hibernate; they just sleep deeply in communal burrows, plugging the entrance with leaves or grass on cold nights.

If you were predisposed to admire skunks from afar, do not waver. Breathe deeply and put away your prejudice. Their musk is the smell of spring, the fragrance of the natural world.

Ode to a Devil's Urn

Most winged and flowering harbingers of spring are weeks away. But now, east of the Rockies, nothing speaks of coming beauty quite like the devil's urn — that black, leathery, edible (though vile-tasting) fungus fruiting on dead hardwoods, cankering living ones, and whose apt Latin name, *Urnula craterium*, translates to "burned crater."

If you look past the physical appearance of this agent of decay and rebirth, you may perceive in its function something more beautiful than any Grecian urn. What's more, you have reason to rejoice if you discover devil's urns on your property, because their presence proves that your soil is fertile. Not only do these fungi herald spring, they symbol-ize it as well, for few forest denizens are so fecund. Spores require about 1½ hours to germinate, and the success rate is extremely high.

If the sight of a March devil's urn buoys your spirits as much as, say, the first flash of a June tanager, then you have arrived as a naturalist.

Grating Chorus

From New Jersey to Florida and west to Oklahoma, an explosion of song is likely to burst forth with late winter's first rains. In grassy swales, moist woodlands, and the marshy margins of ponds and streams, the upland chorus frog — a diminutive tree frog barely larger than a spring peeper — clasps low stems and branches with his sucker

toes, balloons his throat, and carols to the world in a voice best duplicated by running your thumb over a comb's teeth.

At this season, however, it is hard to be critical of the song of any creature spirited enough to make the effort. Be grateful for the grating, and search for a songster far more beautiful than the song. But finding chorus frogs is a major challenge. Stand still until they sing again, then patiently scan ground cover with a muted flashlight. The first feature you see is likely to be the light line along his upper lip; the second, the dark strip from snout to groin.

Winter Birdsong

You'll start to hear it throughout most of our nation as the sun pushes higher into the winter sky — a clear, ringing caroling that comes before almost any other sign of spring — maybe a whistled "purdy, purdy, purdy" or a "cheer, cheer, cheer" or a "whit-chew, whit-chew, whit-chew." It's the song of the northern cardinal, another adaptive species that is thriving and extending its range. But it's not just the male you're hearing; the female counters his notes with loud caroling of her own, eliciting matching notes from her prospective mate. As courtship continues into late winter the male will bring her food, tilting his head to place it in her beak. In response she'll flutter her wings in fledglinglike excitement.

To attract cardinals, put out black sunflower seed and cracked corn. They come to feeders but prefer to forage on the ground.

Beach Drillers

With the full and new moons of March, they hit southern California beaches by the thousands, splashing through the nighttime surf, gaining a beachhead, and digging in. They are grunion — not ruthless invaders from the Isle of Grun, as was postulated in episodes of the old TV sitcom *The Beverly Hillbillies* — but pencil-length, silver fish.

Unlike other fish, grunion leave the water to spawn on land. As the high tide ebbs, the female curves her body and, squeaking, drills herself at least two inches into the wet sand, where she lays as many as 3,000 eggs. Males curl around her, depositing their milt. Eggs remain buried for about two weeks, feeding shorebirds and sandworms, until the next series of high tides release the fry.

Humans chase grunion, dashing down the beach when they show above the wave line. Grunion are superb table fare — best rolled in salted cornmeal or flour and then fried. You are only permitted to catch them with your hands, in March, June, July, and August. People older than 16 need fishing licenses. There is no limit, but use what you take; wasting fish is illegal in California.

Skunk Bear

In tundra and boreal forests of Europe, Russia, Siberia, and Alaska and in the high, wild country of the western United States, most notably central Idaho, winter belongs to the wolverine. This, the largest and least known member of the weasel family, does best where snow remains on the ground for long periods. The wolverine rarely weighs more than 35 pounds, yet it is capable of running down and dispatching elk, reindeer, and mountain sheep. And it can dig through ice and gnaw through frozen carcasses and bones. Because of these adaptations it is often closely attended by foxes. It marks trees in the fashion of bears, clawing and biting bark and perfuming trunks with powerful musk from its anal and ventral glands — behavior that has earned it the alternate name of "skunk bear."

So adept is it at avoiding traps and opening doors, windows, and even cans with its teeth that it has long been supposed to be in league with the devil. Naturalist Ernest Thompson Seton captured the essence of the wolverine when he described it as "a personality of unmeasured force, courage, and achievement so enveloped in a mist of legend, superstition, idolatry, fear, and hatred, that one scarcely knows how to begin or what to accept as fact."

Spring

Spring fever manifests itself in all sorts of ways. For Bill Adamonis — late dean of Yankee "jiggermen" (ice fishermen) — its main symptom was regret. "Spring," he would sigh, as our boots sank into honeycombed ice or the plaintive *Hey, sweetie* of a male chickadee rose from the Cape Cod pitch pines, "always comes so early." But while I have learned to love all seasons and have come to understand that nothing comes "alive" in spring because nothing "dies" in winter, I'm not immune to the giddiness that grips my fellow creatures from rodents to lagomorphs to canids to reptiles to birds, all the way down to humans.

Spring is a grand time for all who love nature and want to learn more about it. But it can be a difficult and confusing time, because everything happens at once. Your senses are bombarded. At 4:30 A.M. you're rousted from sleep by a cacophony of birdsong. Who is saying what? If you look down to admire blooming cowslips, trout lilies, or a freshly undenned snake, a mourning cloak will sail by you at head level. But how can you watch butterflies when the crowns of budding hardwoods are rustling with transient warblers? And how can you concentrate on any of these things when the south wind carries the heady fragrance of wet earth, open marsh, and rambling skunks, and when wood frogs are quacking at you from every vernal pool?

Adding to the confusion of spring are the striking differences between its beginning, middle, and end. Spring — especially in the northern half of the country — should be at least two seasons. Each plant blooms at its own time. Each migratory bird arrives on its own schedule.

Looking at and seeing the natural world is a skill that takes years to acquire. You can learn it and teach it much more effectively if you keep a journal of "firsts" and if, on every expedition, you make a list of notable sightings. Kids respond well to such lists, especially when they're assigned the task of writing down each entry. Even a trip in the car that might have been spent playing video games can just as easily become a natural-history expedition.

"Does that count?" our children would demand, as we passed a gray squirrel. Well, no. It has to be a "notable" sighting. In our yard there's scarcely a time when a squirrel isn't in view. Still, this one might have made the list, had it been alive. The crow that hopped off it, however, was eagerly recorded by Scott. Beth got to record the wood-chuck that, shortly thereafter, rose to survey the traffic from the grassy median. What they were learning was not wild-life identification alone, but the art of looking and seeing.

Never take children on "nature walks." It smacks of the teaching from which they have just been sprung. Take them on "expeditions" instead, and do so with a stated purpose — even if it's bogus. Gather pussy willows, for example; build a house out of sticks and leaves; collect chrysalides; catch pollywogs. The most indelible natural-history lessons are taught by actions, not words.

It took me years to unlearn the lesson taught me by my maternal grandmother, who, on encountering a large snap-ping turtle crossing our island road one long-ago June day, fetched an ax-toting woodsman to separate it from its head. But at Trout Lake camp deep in the woods of Quebec's Eastern Townships, my five-year-old pal Forrest Stearns dashed up to me, grinning proudly and clutching a writhing garter snake — the first we'd encountered that year. She had never considered the possibility that someone might recoil in disgust from snakes, because she had never seen anyone do such a thing. By stopping to admire snakes, her parents had taught her that they are beautiful and special.

Spring bird-watching is an exercise in frustration. Most birds, and especially neotropical migrants, don't hold still long enough to be identified even by people who don't need to flip through field guides. Forget bird-watching then, and take up bird listening. Recordings of the songs and calls of birds you're likely to encounter in your area are available from local Audubon gift shops and birding supply stores. You can even download them over the Internet, if you do a search for "birdsong" or "birding by ear."

In our family the most important events of the new year are not reported by the media. "All news, as it is called, is gossip, and they who edit and read it are old women over their tea," Thoreau correctly observed. For us, genuine "news" is the first appearance of one of the chipmunks that den around the backyard flower garden. Almost always it pops up through corn snow, stretches, sits erect, and gazes around its property. Almost always I am there to see it because the den is just 10 feet from my office window. Other major news events in our household are the first turkey vulture, the first male red-winged blackbird, the first phoebe, the first spring peepers, the first bumblebee, the first painted turtle; later the first catbird, the first towhee; later still the first Baltimore oriole, the first lady's slipper, the first firefly. . . .

One fine, gusty March morning Beth ran back into the classroom from recess to announce monumental news to Miss Smith, her second-grade teacher. The first turkey vulture of the year! "No," intoned Miss Smith. "There are no turkey vultures around here." Beth was puzzled. She had been taught that teachers know best. On the other hand, she had been taught that turkey vultures show up at this time of year in central Massachusetts, that they are large black birds with naked heads and dihedral wings, and that they wobble when they fly. She knew what a turkey vulture looked like as well as she knew what Santa Claus looked like.

"But I saw one," she declared.

"No," said Miss Smith.

Just before school got out for the summer, Miss Smith carefully explained to the class that there was no Santa Claus. Beth was crestfallen to hear this news. While neither she nor Scott had ever met Santa Claus, they had encountered all manner of evidence of his annual visits — chewed-up carrots and ungulate droppings on the porch roof, presents accidentally dropped on the roof and addressed to other children — which Scott and Beth were allowed to play with for exactly one year until the following Christmas Eve when they had to return them to Santa with explanatory notes, never to see them again.

When Beth informed me that there was no Santa Claus, I asked her how she had arrived at this conclusion.

"Miss Smith told me," she said.

"Well of course Miss Smith doesn't believe in Santa Claus," I responded. "She doesn't even believe in turkey vultures."

Beth thought for a moment. "Oh yeah," she said.

A Mewing of Catbirds

With robins extending their winter range ever northward, the gray catbird has taken over as the true harbinger of spring east of the Rockies. The males come first in congregations aptly called "mewings" — from the catlike complaint that terminates their rambling, melodious, often nocturnal songs in which vocalizations of any of at least 100 birds may be mimicked. One catbird that resided near a cemetery where "Taps" was frequently played learned the notes of the first three phrases.

"Catbirds," observed by early-twentieth-century ornithologist Chester Reed, "seem determined to find out what you are doing, why you are doing it, and what you are going to do next. . . . It is in turn a merry jester, a fine musician, a mocking sprite, and a screaming termagant." And no other bird provides a better excuse for not mowing or pruning, because thickets thus preserved provide nesting sites.

Watch the wild courtship chases, and listen to the outpouring of song. Puffed up and tail lowered, the male bows until his bill touches the ground, lifts his tail, sashays, struts, and flashes his chestnut rump patch. Both sexes construct several "practice nests," but the final one is usually built by the female. She will almost always eject cowbird eggs; but on rare occasions her first egg will quickly be dumped by the cowbird; and she will then misidentify and eject her own eggs.

Golden Harbinger

If you thought the first bright wildflower of spring was a small dandelion, look closer. It's probably coltsfoot — a diminutive, look-alike relative from Eurasia and Africa that's now naturalized in most of America. Officially, it's a weed, but in the bleakness of early spring one has difficulty generating much antipathy toward the gaudy, golden blooms bravely pushing through mud and snow.

Oddly, the flowers die before the horse-hoof-shaped leaves appear, a trait that convinced early botanists that the plant was leafless. Both flower and leaves have been used as cough medicine for at least 2,000 years. The silk crowning the seed heads is favored as nesting material by chickadees and goldfinches.

Dance of the Fiddleheads

As snow and shadows shrink on forest and meadow, ferns pop through the wet earth. You've seen these "fiddleheads" bending back and forth as they unfurl in slow-motion nature films. But if you look at a plant each day at the same hour and make a crude sketch on paper or in your mind, you can see the unfurling in real time. The speed will astonish you. In diverse array over most of the globe, ferns — some of them 50 feet high — helped build Earth's oxygen-rich atmosphere ages before the first flowering plants existed.

For centuries it was supposed that ferns were flowering plants, but that they bloomed so rarely no one saw the blossoms. Long, futile vigils were kept, and it became widely believed that if the seeds were collected at midnight, the possessor could not be perceived by human eyes. ("We have the receipt of fern-seed," effuses Gadshill in Shakespeare's *Henry IV, Part 1.* "We walk invisible.") When the microscope was invented, fern watchers discovered something nearly as magical — spores so tiny they could float in the air, wafting across oceans.

Fiddleheads of the ostrich fern are delicious. They should be cut without much stem, cleaned of their brown scales, boiled for about two minutes, then sautéed with garlic, chives, and butter.

Spring Cure-All

These days the main and best use of hepatica is for brightening late-winter woodlands just about everywhere in America and, with them, the spirits of those afflicted with cabin fever. You have to admire any wildflower with the pluck to bloom under corn snow. But combine this with blossoms that vary between white, lavender, pink, and blue, all in pastels as delicate as the season is harsh, and you have what John Burroughs called "the gem of the woods."

Hepatica is also used (with declining frequency) to treat sunburn, freckles, bleeding lungs, and, since its leaves are shaped like a liver, ailments of that organ. Seventeenth-century English herbalist Nicholas Culpeper recommended it for "bites of mad-dogs." Native Americans used it to straighten crossed eyes and expel — albeit with the contents of their stomachs — dreams about snakes.

A Wondrous Bird

On the ground or in bushes or trees along all three coasts north to southern California and North Carolina, brown pelicans are building nests of sticks, reeds, and grass. The next time bad news about native fauna plunges you into a funk, consider this bird's recent history. Because brown pelicans incubate eggs with their feet, thereby placing a lot of weight on them, the shells were especially vulnerable to breaking when thinned by DDT and other hard pesticides. As a result the species nearly went extinct. By 1966, the year Louisiana made it its official bird, the brown pelican had essentially vanished from the state.

Recovery after banning DDT has been spectacular: in 2009 the brown pelican was removed from the federal endangered species list. This, the smallest pelican, is the only one that's brown and the only one that procures prey by plunge diving.

Though rarely celebrated for his scientific acuity, poet Dixon Lanier Merritt had it right when he observed: *"Oh, a wondrous bird is the pelican/ His beak will hold more than his belican."* The capacity of the brown pelican's pouch, in fact, exceeds that of its belly by a factor of three. But Merritt erred with: *"He can take in his beak/food enough for a week."* The bird uses its pouch merely as a net, always carrying prey in its gullet.

Backyard Wolves

When snowpacks shrink and the wet earth stirs with insect life, hungry wolf spiders — common most everywhere on the planet, especially in the United States — emerge from their dens and burrows. These stout, hairy arachnids can reach two inches in length. All 3,000 known species lack the ability to spin webs; instead, they pursue their prey, sometimes running it down like wolves (though not in packs), sometimes ambushing it like cougars.

Eight prominent eyes allow a wolf spider to take in the scene above and behind. A male courts a female by tapping the ground and waving his front legs and two armlike, sperm-transferring appendages, called pedipalps, at her. The female totes her eggs in a sac, and when the young emerge they may ride on her back.

Spring Quackers

How can there be so many ducks in that tiny puddle of snowmelt? Tiptoe toward it, and instantly the quacking ceases. Yet there is no explosion of wings — only the faintest of ripples and the rustle of budding trees in the March breeze. Where are the ducks? Not here, because these vocalists are male wood frogs — handsome fellows wearing brown waistcoats and rakish black masks, who distinguish themselves among frogs by singing by day as well as night.

Take a seat, and after 15 or 20 minutes they'll start again, their double vocal sacs flashing white with each inflation. As many as five males will grasp a larger, redder female, occasionally killing her in their ardor. Eggs, floating in apple-size masses and attached to vegetation or resting on the bottom, hatch quickly, because vernal pools are short-lived.

Wood frogs are largely terrestrial, inhabiting moist north country and/or high country all the way to the Arctic Circle and beyond — farther north than any other reptile or amphibian. Antifreeze in their blood protects them from sudden cold snaps. Permafrost defines the northern limit of their range, preventing them from hibernating in the mud.

Shaggy Fur, Smooth Stones

We don't have much room for North America's largest land animal anymore. So a female bison facing into the prairie wind and licking the wet fur of her new calf in early spring is a sight to lift the spirits of all who love wildness. An hour after birth the calf will be standing; it will be running in four hours.

We almost lost them. The last eastern bison was killed in Pennsylvania in 1799; the last free-ranging herd of western plains bison (before limited restoration got under way in Yellowstone) was destroyed in Montana in 1891.

Bison scratch themselves on large, hard objects, which were at a premium in their realm before it was defiled by iron rail. Here and there on the Great Plains you'll see huge, polished boulders standing in depressions — perhaps behind a shopping mall. They were rough-edged when the glacier cast them off, but millions of bison rumps and flanks over 10,000 years wore them smooth; the depressions were made by their hooves.

These boulders are monuments to America's lost wealth. Look for them later; now it's spring, and there's new life on the prairie.

Toxic Toes

Even before grass appears, plains, open woodlands, and railroad rights-of-way in our upper Midwest and south to Texas brighten with sundry shades of indigo as prairie larkspur opens its blossoms to bumblebee pollinators and late-spring sun. A mature plant may stand close to four feet high and support as many as 30 flowers on a 10-inch spike. The name "larkspur" derives from the projection at the back of each flower that resembles the hind toe of a bird.

Prairie larkspur belongs to the family Ranunculaceae, named for Ranunculus — a figure in Greek mythology noted for his colorful clothing. Even more impressive was his singing, which dazzled everyone, including himself. One day, while crooning to some wood nymphs, he became so excited by his own voice that he expired in the middle of his song, whereupon the magical musician Orpheus converted him to a flower.

Prairie larkspur is unpopular with ranchers because it is deadly to cattle, which seem unable to avoid eating it. But at least in earlier times, it partially redeemed itself by killing lice and nits when rubbed into one's hair.

Flight of the Bumblebee

A bumblebee may not be the first insect you see in spring, but it's likely to be the first you hear. *"The sound of [the] buzz,"* offers poet Mary O'Neill, *"is a rick-racky singsong / Muffled in fuzz."* It starts suddenly on some hushed day in late winter over snow-bent grass or along the sun-washed side of your house where the wet earth splits over swelling bulbs. Never will you see bumblebees bigger than the ones you see now, for they are queens laden with fertilized eggs — the sole survivors from last autumn.

A queen's flight is not wild and erratic, as Rimsky-Korsakov's operatic score would imply, but slow, low, and purposeful. She is searching for a nest site — an abandoned chipmunk burrow, perhaps — which she'll stuff and camouflage with grass, moss, and leaves. Next she'll make a wax pot the size of a thimble and fill it with honey; finally, she'll knead pollen and nectar into a loaf of "bee bread." The

honey will sustain her while she's brooding, and the larvae will eat the bread. Six of North America's 51 bumblebee species are parasitic — cowbird analogues whose queens lay eggs in nests of other species and let the workers rear the young.

The bumblebee's dense hair allows it to live in colder

climates than most other flying insects. Colonies have been found 545 miles from the North Pole. We are particularly fond of our bumblebees, for reasons both obvious and elusive: They are harbingers of fine weather, they resemble winged teddy bears, and they are so good-natured that getting one to sting you is a major undertaking.

But most important, perhaps, they are ours; unlike honeybees, they are native to the continent.

Drummer in the Woods

Almost everywhere in wooded North America, spring begins with a loud, two-second drumroll. If you can count the beats, chances are it's a downy woodpecker. If you can't, it's probably a hairy woodpecker — the downy's larger, longer-billed cousin.

The colossal noise issuing from the diminutive, black-and-white downy is a declaration of territory and a means of staying in touch with its mate. When downies feed on insects in deadwood and under bark, however, you can barely hear the tapping.

Both male and female will drum on any resonant surface, including clapboards and rain gutters. When they select a metal roof, they can be as loud as jackhammers. At first light and a few feet from a person's bed, such serenades can infuriate even bird lovers. But have patience; courtship is brief as spring.

White Reprise

As the last patches of snow finally shrink under a high, lingering sun, the woods turn white again. In rich forestland from Ontario and Quebec and south to Arkansas and Georgia, large-flowered trilliums are in full bloom. Like all trilliums, they have three leaves, three sepals, three petals, and a three-chambered pistil. Other common varieties include the painted trillium — so called for the fuchsia veins in the center of its white, wavy-edged petals — and the aptly named stinking Benjamin, or wet-dog trillium, which seems to be appreciated by only its carrion-fly pollinators.

Trilliums have evolved a unique method of dispersal. In late summer the capsule containing the seeds splits open, spilling them on the ground. Attached to each seed is a crest composed of a sweet material relished by ants. Ants drag away the crest with its attached seed, then eat the former and discard the latter.

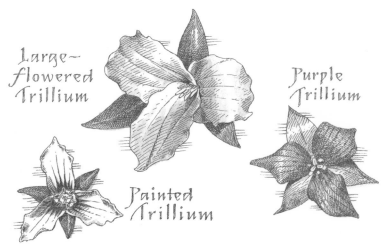

Large-flowered Trillium

Purple Trillium

Painted Trillium

Sky Flakes

Robert Frost called them "sky flakes" and "flowers that fly and all but sing." When the last corn snow is a puddle on the greening earth, they start emerging from overwintering pupae to skip through woodlands, fields, prairies, and backyards from Pacific to Atlantic and Gulf to tundra's edge. They are azures — quarter-size butterflies, usually dusted with cobalt scales.

Some field guides have the taxonomy wrong; lepidopterists have recently discovered that what they had been calling the "spring azure" may be at least half a dozen species. There is indeed a spring azure — one of our earliest emerging butterflies, whose flight period wanes in early May and whose pupae go directly into diapause until the following spring. Then there is the slightly duller summer azure that, in most of its range, starts flying in June and produces up to three generations before its last flight in autumn. This is the one you're likely to see in treeless areas and city parks.

Among other recently discovered species are the cherry-gall azure, the coastal holly azure, and the hops azure. If you see a diminutive blue butterfly between the flight periods of spring and summer azures, catch it. You may have a new species.

Sexy Snakes

Among the first reptiles to emerge from winter's hibernation in the Northeast is the handsome striped or checkered eastern garter snake — also and more aptly called garden snake. As the northern hemisphere leans into the sun, sex — not food — is the garter's first priority. It's not uncommon to see a female pursued by a dozen males. In late summer 12 to 40 young are born alive.

To find this most common of suburban reptiles you often don't have to look beyond your front steps, provided there is space underneath and they are in full sunlight. Garters eat fish, frogs, tadpoles, earthworms, insects, and toads, whose poison doesn't affect them. While birds are often eaten by snakes, with garters it's the other way around. Hawks and owls glut themselves on them, and it is not unusual to see young robins and jays with the wiggling tails of baby garters protruding from their beaks.

Especially when cold, garter snakes are adept at flattening themselves out and appearing and acting vicious and viperlike. But it's all bluff; the gravest danger is getting squirted with foul-smelling musk when you pick them up.

The Vulture Test

Poets commonly celebrate the first robin and bluebird of the year, not the first black vulture. This cousin to the stork — an "antistork," symbolizing death instead of procreation — is a bald-headed scavenger drawn flylike to filth, that gorges on rotting offal, that cools and disinfects its legs by hosing them down with acidic excreta, that hisses and grunts if you startle it on the ground, then projectile vomits into your face. So if your heart soars at the sight of the first black vulture of spring, you have arrived as a naturalist.

You may spy a black vulture almost anywhere in the United States, but most likely in the Southeast. Black vultures will roust larger turkey vultures from carrion. They flap more than turkey vultures, lack their red heads, and are aloft later in the day and on straighter wings.

One poet who *did* celebrate the black vulture was George Sterling:

Aloof upon the day's immeasured dome,
    He holds unshared the silence of the sky.
    Far down his bleak, relentless eyes descry
The eagle's empire and the falcon's home.

Spicing Up Spring

Before most other plants bloom, the pale, yellow flowers of northern spicebush brighten low, deciduous woods from Texas to Kansas and east to the Atlantic states. The nectar sustains all manner of pollinators, and the leaves are the larval food source for the spectacular spicebush swallowtail butterfly. You'll have to look hard for these caterpillars because they roll themselves up in the leaves. When you find one, note the two dorsal eyespots that make it look like a snake, presumably to intimidate would-be predators.

In autumn at least 20 species of birds feed on the spicebush's red berries. These fruits can be dried and used for spice, and a tea can be made from the leaves. Northern spicebush, readily available at nurseries, is ideal for gardens, especially rain gardens that utilize roof runoff. And as with other native plants and unlike so many exotic ornamentals, you can plant it and, apart from occasional weeding and trimming, pretty much forget about it.

Slow-Motion Monster

Early spring is the best time to see one of the few monsters recognized by science — a resident not of lochs or seas but of the deserts of our Southwest. The Gila monster, our largest lizard, spends 98 percent of its time underground. But now, especially early in the day, it waddles about looking for eggs, young birds, and young mammals. At a maximum size of five pounds and 24 inches, it's a thoroughly unimpressive "monster," but it is one of only two descendants of the venomous lizards that roamed Earth 40 million years ago.

Its poison, about as potent as that of a rattlesnake, is chewed into the victim; but there isn't much, and it is almost never fatal to people. Unlike rattlesnakes, Gila monsters use their venom strictly for defense, delivering it as a last resort after hissing and backing away. Moreover, they're so sluggish they almost require human help in the human-biting process.

If you get bitten, it serves you right — at least according to one Dr. Ward who, in the September 23, 1899, *Arizona Graphic*, vented his spleen as follows: "I have never been called to attend a case of Gila monster bite, and I don't want to be. I think a man who is fool enough to get bitten by a Gila monster ought to die."

Damsels and Dragons

Two hundred and fifty million years ago, even before the rise of dinosaurs, they patrolled steaming Carboniferous swamps on veined, translucent wings. As other life-forms vanished from our planet, these ancient predators prospered; today there are few places on Earth where you can't find at least one of some of the 5,000 species of Odonata — damselflies and their close relatives, dragonflies.

Dragonflies have enormous eyes, while the eyes of damselflies are smaller and set more widely apart. Unlike dragonflies, which keep their wings open while resting, damselflies hold their wings together over their backs.

With the first warm days of spring, Odonata nymphs crawl out of still and flowing water, climb whatever's handy, and emerge as adults through splits in their skin. Look for them before they take flight as they rest beside their cast-off nymphal skins, pumping hardening fluid from their bloated bodies into veins in their still-soft wings.

Soon they'll be hawking insects and, according to some sources, showing good boys where the pickerel are and sewing the lips of bad ones shut.

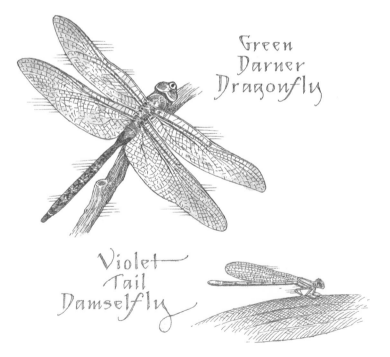

Green Darner Dragonfly

Violet Tail Damselfly

Loon Music

Common loons, fresh from their ocean wintering habitat along the Pacific, Gulf, and Atlantic coasts, from the Aleutians to Newfoundland, are chasing spring toward the tree line, ditching into lakes like stricken bombers, kicking up spray and skidding sideways. Sometimes they arrive minutes after ice-out, a feat they accomplish with constant reconnaissance flights.

Watch these goose-size birds as they thrash the water in their defensive "penguin dance" or as they hunt for fish, ruby eyes submerged, black-and-white-checkered bodies floating high or low, depending on how much air they've squeezed from their feathers. Perhaps you will see one flash under your canoe, propelling itself with enormous webbed feet.

Then, when the spires of the boreal forest blot the sun, listen to their music. It will start at one end of the lake and rush to the other — a wild, discordant yodeling like the thunder of expanding ice, a tremolo of demented laughter, somewhere a single, gentle hoot, or perhaps a wail like the distant whistle of a southbound freight. The yodel is the territorial vocalization of the male, actually the song. The wail and hoot are contact calls to family members; the tremolo, uttered in flight as well as on the water, connotes alarm.

For those seeking respite from things human, few prescriptions are more curative than loon music. It is best taken when lying on one's back under bright stars and beside campfire smoke that rises straight, with the music itself, into the infinite northern night.

Miner's Cat

In the southwest quarter of the country male ringtail cats are rubbing urine into the ground and onto raised objects. While such scent-post marking is standard behavior throughout the year, now it becomes a method of attracting prospective mates as well as deterring competing males. Ringtail cats are not felines but slender, diminutive cousins of the raccoon. Like raccoons they are largely nocturnal; and they're even more arboreal, leaping nimbly among branches, instantly reversing direction, even performing cartwheels. This agility is derived from sharp, semiretractile claws; a long, heavy tail that aides in balance; and hind feet that rotate 180 degrees.

Ringtails are meticulous groomers. After eating or sleeping they'll sit catlike on their haunches, cleaning fur with tongue and forepaws. Capture a ringtail, and it will scream loudly and douse you with vile-smelling musk from its anal glands. Such rocky introductions notwithstanding, ringtails are easily tamed — a fact not lost on early miners and other settlers who kept them to control mice, making warm daytime dens for their pets out of wooden boxes they placed beside the woodstove. The ringtail's talent for mousing, which far exceeds that of a domestic cat, earned it the alternate name "miner's cat."

Muskrat Love

In every contiguous state and north to Arctic tundra, muskrats are beginning their long, productive breeding season. Four times the size of Norway rats but stockier and with rounder ears and blunter faces, they are really aquatic voles. And like other voles, they are primarily herbivores, consuming a wide variety of marsh plants with occasional side dishes of mussels, crayfish, frogs, and turtles.

On still nights listen for the squeaky vocalization of the courting female, approximated with surprising accuracy in the pop song "Muskrat Love." Where there is still ice, you'll see muskrats popping up through the dome-shaped "push-ups" they have maintained all winter. In warmer latitudes look for them at the apex of the Vs they carve on moonlit or starlit water, as they paddle with outward-turned feet, steering with vertically flattened tails, heads, and rumps above the surface, pushing silver wedges of "bow wake."

Birding by Ear

Great billows of warblers are now rustling through eastern hardwood forests — quick, gaudy birds representing some 50 species. From South and Central America they follow the green, insect-rich edge of spring, wafting across the Yucatán Peninsula to the Gulf Coast, blowing up the Mississippi, the Appalachians, and the Atlantic seaboard.

Forget trying to identify them all visually. They move too fast and feed too high. You'll have better luck learning their distinctive songs from recordings produced by the Cornell Laboratory of Ornithology. After a southwest wind watch the weather for localized rainstorms, which can force down night migrants, instantly filling bare woodlands with caroling and color. Get there before first light because some of the unusual warblers may sing only for the first hour.

Teddy Bears' Picnic

Black-bear cubs — as many as four to a litter and usually born in early February — emerge from their dens in spring, but unlike their mothers, they have not been hibernating. Instead, they have been nursing as she slept. Now the size of small tabby cats, they are in fine flesh and frolicking in a new universe of sights, smells, sounds, and tastes. Their mother will tend them for almost a year and a half, then drive them away.

If you encounter a black-bear family in the wild, keep your distance but consider yourself blessed, not threatened. Because black bears evolved in forested habitats, they almost always react to danger by running away or climbing a tree. Our other two bear species — grizzlies and polar bears — evolved on open ground and therefore are more likely to stand and fight.

Land clearing and unrestricted hunting in the late 1800s devastated black-bear populations over most of the United States. But under modern wildlife management and with the regrowth of their forest habitat, the species is making a dramatic comeback.

Merry Thieves

Along the Atlantic and Gulf coasts laughing gulls are incubating eggs or feeding newly hatched young. Now the parents have shed their drab winter plumage and sport handsome black hoods, white arcs around the eyes, black wing tips, and red bills and legs.

There are few things laughing gulls won't eat. Noisy, quarrelsome swarms follow fishing boats and ferries, feasting on bycatch and lunch items respectively. They'll consume berries, pick flying ants off the water and out of the air, and orbit dock lights at night, hawking moths.

What laughing gulls lack in fishing skill they make up for in aptitude for thievery. Their calls, similar to human laughter, set the mood at seaside restaurants. Answering guffaws from a human diner may accompany the first (rarely the second) theft of a French fry from plate or fork. Even ornithologists have a hard time being clinical when they observe what they call "kleptoparasitism." A laughing gull will alight on a pelican's head, and as the pelican opens its beak to dump water and reposition its catch, the gull will reach in and help itself.

Jill-in-the-Pulpit

If you've left any bootprints in low, wet places along the eastern coastal plain and piedmont, you've probably encountered the jack-in-the-pulpit. This cousin of the skunk cabbage is named for the hood that serves as an umbrella, protecting flowers and pollen and resembling the baffle of an old-fashioned pulpit. "Jack" is the clublike, flower-bearing spadix within.

What you might not have realized is that there are female jack-in-the-pulpits, known as jills, and that a usually one-leafed jack will change into a usually two-leafed jill if growing conditions are good. Jills change back into jacks when growing conditions worsen. To distinguish the sex, gently lift the hood. If the flowers deep inside look like threads, you've got a jack. If they resemble tiny green berries, you've got a jill.

These ubiquitous spring wildflowers transplant well, but the stress tends to turn jills into jacks. Better to wait till late summer and collect the red berries for planting.

River Dance

How lifeless seem the rivers and rills that meet the cold Atlantic in mud time. All that moves within them are caddis fly larvae shuffling over stone and log or perhaps the brown carcasses of last year's water milfoil and coontail waving languidly in the swollen current. Then, in a storm of protein from the sea, come the river herring. In pools below the outfalls of ancient mill dams and rickety fishways, they spiral like galaxies, swollen with eggs and milt, spooking themselves, dashing down-current, then returning and holding again until the town herring warden releases water for their upstream journey.

River herring is the collective name for two nearly identical species occurring along most of the East Coast: the alewife and the slightly sleeker, smaller-eyed blueback herring, which starts its spawning run a few weeks later. Don't walk by a coastal stream without looking. Mostly they pass unseen, save by herons hunched over the pools like old men in ratty down jackets standing at a truck-stop counter.

Pretender to the Throne

Weeks before monarchs breed their way north, a mimic butterfly appears around the newly lush margins of lakes, rivers, and swamps from central Canada, through most of the United States, and into Mexico. Unlike monarchs, which migrate south, viceroys winter as partially grown larvae, protected by antifreeze in their blood and by the hibernacula they construct with silk and rolled-up leaves and enter headfirst. When they emerge in spring, they're still larvae, but they quickly pupate.

Study the adult, and the differences between it and the monarch become less subtle. The pretender is smaller and faster, glides on horizontal rather than dihedral wings, and has a thin black band across the dark veins of its hind wings.

Most monarchs are unpalatable to birds, a fact that apparently explains the evolutionary strategy behind the viceroy's appearance. For years it was believed that birds would relish viceroys if they'd try them, but recent evidence suggests that viceroys, too, are distasteful. "Presumably, a greater number of similar-looking, unpalatable individuals in an area results in a faster learning curve for birds," writes lepidopterist Jeffrey Glassberg.

Sky Dance

While robins bask in the South, woodcocks waft north by night until, backlit against the dawn, they flutter mothlike into brushy draws from the Maritimes to the southern Appalachians and west to the Great Plains. The woodcock is an upland snipe — a strange, gnomelike bird with stubby legs, a brain that lies almost upside down, high-set eyes that give better vision above and behind, and a long bill equipped with a hinged upper mandible, the better to grasp worms.

Just before dusk, take a seat in an overgrown pasture, and you may witness the mating display of the male. When the light fades you'll hear a nasal "peeent," then another and another, closer and closer together until at last, with a twitter of wings, he launches into the twilight. The twittering rises and falls as he orbits under the first stars of evening, sometimes climbing to 300 feet. Presently the twittering gives way to a liquid warble, and he drops earthward, slicing and dipping like an oak leaf. At the last possible instant, he levels off and glides back to his spot. Then, strutting with drooped wings and spread tail, he resumes his singing and, soon, his sky dance.

Underdogs

Remove the black-tailed prairie dog from its niche in our western plains and — as Americans have discovered over the past century — the whole biota collapses like the sides of a stone arch. This ground squirrel, whose "dog" name derives from its bark, is called a keystone species because it provides food and / or habitat for at least 59 vertebrate species — 29 birds, 21 mammals, 5 reptiles, and 4 amphibians.

The elaborate subterranean design of a prairie-dog town includes bedrooms, latrines, birthing and nursing chambers, pantries, even cemeteries. In May look for youngsters as they stumble up into the sunlight for the first time in their six-week lives. Soon they'll be roughhousing, grooming each other, and greeting neighbors with chirps, hugs, and open-mouthed "kisses."

Because prairie dogs eat forbs and grasses, they have been widely poisoned and shot in the mistaken belief that they compete with livestock. Studies, however, show that in aerating and turning over the soil they produce high-quality forage.

Underwater Artist

If the United States had a national fish, it would be the ubiquitous bluegill sunfish, alias "kivver" or "sunny" — a native or transplant in ponds, lakes, and dawdling streams almost everywhere in our nation. In May — when the belly of the male turns sunrise orange — he eases into the shallows to scoop out a plate-size depression with his tail in sand, mud, gravel, or clay. Then, with the flair of a French impressionist, he adds a leaf here, a stick or pine needle there. Step onto the masterpiece with your bare feet, and you're apt to get bitten on the toe by the volatile but toothless artist.

He fertilizes the female's eggs as she deposits them in his nest; then he guards them jealously. When they hatch, he protects the fry for almost a week, until they have absorbed their yolk sacs and struck out on their own. Few freshwater fish provide better table fare than bluegills, and none is easier to catch. Usually that is a prescription for disaster, but so prolific is this species that the main management challenge is thinning out populations to prevent stunting.

Water Moths

Part of the twilight magic of streams and ponds are caddis flies, mothlike insects that emerge from daylight retreats to hover and dip or skate over the surface, sometimes vanishing into silver craters made by rising trout. Throughout North America, 1,400 known species representing 26 families come in a variety of dimensions and colors — from the size of gnats to the size of dragonflies, and in most every shade of brown, yellow, and green.

Spring is the best time for watching both adults and larvae. Get to the water when there's still plenty of light, then study the bottom. Eventually, you'll see little "sticks" and "pebbles" moving over logs and stones. Pick them up and you'll find they are aquatic "caterpillars" that have encased themselves in sand or bits of wood, shell, or other detritus. They feed on algae or carrion. A few forms don't build protective cases but hunt prey or catch it in tunnel-shaped webs they weave with silk.

Embracing Rattlesnakes

If you live east of the Mississippi, mid-April through mid-May is the time to look for timber rattlesnakes as they emerge from hibernation dens in south-facing cliffs and boulder fields. Which brings up the question: Why would you want to? Maybe because these stocky pit vipers are beautiful, secretive, and rare to the point of being semi-mythical. In Maine, Rhode Island, Michigan, and Delaware they've not been seen in recent years and may have been extirpated — all the more reason to look for them there.

Timber rattlers vary from almost jet black to yellow with brown or black blotches on their sides and back. In the southern part of their range, a chestnut stripe may run along their backs. So shy are these snakes that if you encounter one, it will almost certainly be by your choice. And so docile are they that getting one to strike you requires major effort.

Love of timber rattlers is a new cultural phenomenon in America. As recently as 1989, for example, Minnesota was paying a bounty on them. In Wisconsin, where the bounty was discontinued in 1975, one exterminator reported killing 5,700 in a single season.

Wrongs to Rights

Cruising underwater for a third of an hour, then punching through the surface to take four to six short breaths, female right whales and their young are migrating from calving grounds off Florida and Georgia to summer range off New England and the Maritimes. These are northern right whales; and while two other subspecies (the southern right and north Pacific right) are recognized, all are strikingly similar.

Right whales, the first cetaceans to be commercially exploited, got their name because they were slow, easily pursued, and floated when dead — ergo, the "right" whale to kill. Heads, a quarter of the body length, are splotched with "callosities" — crusty skin growths housing whale lice that graze on dead tissue. Unlike most other whales, rights lack dorsal fins.

It is not clear why, after 70 years of protection, the species still flirts with extinction while others, such as grays, humpbacks, and sperms, have rebounded. One possible explanation is that right whales are slow and ponderous and therefore especially vulnerable to ship strikes and entanglement by fishing gear.

Big Noise, Little Bird

Now, from woodland edges and brushy thickets all across America, comes a bubbling, musical torrent that rises frantically — as if the singer had too many notes and too little time. Abruptly, the music gives way to a harsh, scolding buzz. All this racket issues from the thumb-size house wren, or "jenny wren." There he is on the birdhouse, a tiny gray sprite, stump tail cocked jauntily, sassing the world. His Ojibwe (Chippewa) name means "making big noise for its size."

The male constructs as many as seven nests of twigs in natural cavities or birdhouses, then takes the female on a guided tour, fluttering in front of her and popping in and out of his creations. When she selects her home — usually in mid-May — she sometimes adds more twigs, then builds a deep, soft cup with such material as grass, feathers, or cocoons.

The Turtle Stomp

If you are abroad in the spring woods anywhere from the lake states to the Maritimes and south to Iowa and Virginia, you may encounter the wood turtle, named less for its habitat than its spectacular carapace, which looks as if it had been carved from black walnut. Depending on date and latitude, your wood turtle may be newly emerged from hibernation and easing over the bed of an ice-girded stream or high and dry — positioned under an evergreen canopy to catch a shaft of sunlight no wider than itself. You may even find a courting couple, the male swinging his head atop the female's carapace.

If a turtle is walking on land, follow. Unlike other pond turtles, this species spends much of its life foraging in uplands. It will pause, stretch its orange neck, then daintily pluck a mushroom, berry, or dandelion. Occasionally it will stop, stomp its feet, bang its yellow plastron on the wet earth, then snatch the earthworms brought to the surface by the vibrations. If it's a female, it may be en route to an open, sunny spot to lay eggs.

Illegal collecting threatens the species' existence. In one study, marked specimens began disappearing immediately after the public was invited into a 2,471-acre reservoir watershed. Eight years later only 14 remained. Nine years later they were gone.

Hungry Herbs

Where our southeastern coastal plain slouches into swamps, bogs, and wet prairies, otherworldly predators, sometimes a yard tall, are starting their eight-month hunting season. From southern Virginia to Florida and north to Mississippi they sway in the wind like charmed cobras. They are yellow pitcher plants — carnivorous herbs that compensate for their nutrient-impoverished, usually acidic habitat by devouring insects.

Now petals appear on yet-leafless stalks, and glands pump out aroma attractive to pollinating insects but so reminiscent of cat urine that displays at flower shows have been moved to breezeways. Save for the pollinators that stay high in the reproductive parts and a few large insects, such as wasps, that occasionally chew their way out, there is no escape. Seeking nectar that contains hemlocklike toxin, victims venture down the pitcher's throat, where stiff, downward-pointing hairs guide them lower and where a waxy secretion makes them lose their footing and fall into a digestive stew of enzymes and bacteria.

Lords of the Dance

As the ice recedes north, usually in May, the lords of the dance fly in from southern and coastal waters to breed on lakes in the American and Canadian West. Often you first perceive them by their splashing as they race across the surface, wings back, white breasts protruding, long necks curved, bills thrust above their ruby eyes. There can be two or more dancers, of the same or different sexes. After the dance, partners sometimes pluck weeds and shake them in each other's faces.

Such is the elegant courtship of the western grebe and the Clark's grebe, which overlap in range and are nearly identical save for the latter's brighter yellow bill and smaller black cap. Like anhingas and herons, these birds spear fish with their long bills. They build nests by anchoring aquatic plants to reeds, and when there are 100 or more pairs in a colony, their nests can form a floating island.

Gaudy Undertakers

In spring our largest carrion-eating insect, the inch-and-a-half-long, black-and-orange American burying beetle, emerges from the earth, where it has spent the winter as a pupa, and starts scanning the countryside with antennae that can detect decaying flesh a mile away. A male will fly to a carcass at night, then emit powerful pheromones that attract females. Lying on its back and using its legs like a conveyer belt, a beetle can move a creature 200 times its weight. Working together, a mated pair buries the carcass, clips off fur or feathers, and injects it with preservatives. This done, the female excavates a nearby nursery in which she lays 10 to 30 eggs. Both adults attend the larvae, which rear up and beg for food, stroking their parents' jaws like wolf pups and thereby inducing them to regurgitate.

Burying beetles, federally listed as endangered, used to occur in at least 35 states but now are restricted to parts of Arkansas, Kansas, Nebraska, Oklahoma, South Dakota, Rhode Island, and Massachusetts. Their decline may be linked to extinction of prime food sources — the heath hen along the Atlantic coastal plain and elsewhere the passenger pigeon, thought to have been more numerous than all other North American birds combined. Currently they're being depressed by a proliferation of competing scavengers such as skunks, raccoons, and opossums, and threatened further by climate change.

Mini Monsters

From Arkansas to the Pacific and from British Columbia to
Guatemala, horned lizards — magnified monsters of choice
in 1950s horror flicks — are emerging from hibernation.
Most taxonomists recognize 14 North American species
inhabiting dry areas from oak-pine forests to thorn-scrub
deserts. All horned lizards (or "horny toads," as they are also
called) have wide, flat, spine-fringed bodies and tails, and
heads crowned with sharp, demonlike horns; few adults are
more than seven inches long.

Especially at this time of year, these reptiles can be
seen basking, their backs tracking the sun like solar panels.
At night they stay warm by digging into the dirt, first cutting a trench with their snouts, then enlarging it with their
sides. When it rains they tilt their heads down so that water
runs off their backs and into their mouths. When set upon
by predators, they inflate their bodies like blowfish and, if
pressed, squirt streams of blood from the corners of their
eyes for distances of several feet.

For these "tears of blood" Mexicans call horned lizards *torito de la Virgen* or the Virgin's little bull. Apparently the blood causes discomfort in attackers. A cat, thus anointed, was seen to froth at the mouth and roll.

Hard-Drinking Woodpeckers

East of the Rockies, yellow-bellied sapsuckers are moving north as sap rises in some 250 species of native tree favored by these furtive, medium-size woodpeckers. Listen for the drumming courtship duets of both sexes and watch for the horizontal lines of squarish holes, all pointed slightly downward to collect sap. After a sapsucker has excavated a tree, it will leave to work on another, then return and lick the sap with its brushlike tongue, tilting its head back as if swigging beer.

Describing one feeding bird, nineteenth- and early-twentieth-century naturalist John Burroughs wrote: "Then, when the day was warm, and the sap ran freely, he would have a regular sugar-maple debauch, sitting there by his wells hour after hour, and as fast as they became filled, sipping out the sap." Yellow-bellied sapsuckers guard their holes, squealing angrily at other birds and chasing them away. You can occasionally attract them with suet, peanut butter, or even hummingbird feeders, and they will nest in bluebird boxes.

Azure Acres

Only, perhaps, if the Civil War had been lost by the North would Virginia be large enough to contain all of our Virginia bluebells. From New York to Minnesota and south to Arkansas and North Carolina, these tall, striking forget-me-nots are in spectacular bloom. Sometimes the inch-long, trumpet-shaped flowers extend in azure carpets over acres of floodplain, moist woods, and wet meadow.

Bluebells are ephemeral perennials, which means their foliage begins to die shortly after they bloom. Enjoy them while they last; in a few weeks they'll be completely dormant.

Out Where the Toadies Bawl

The "dogies" you hear bawling now in low, wet places from Nevada to the East Coast aren't necessarily bovines. If they sound a little hoarse and if they start up at dusk or in the dark, they're probably Woodhouse's toads. Named for the nineteenth-century explorer, surgeon, and naturalist Samuel Woodhouse, who first collected them, these large amphibians can be distinguished from the more familiar American toad by their webbed feet and white bellies.

After a hard rain they move into puddles where the males inflate their balloonlike vocal sacs and call in females. A female will lay as many as 28,000 eggs held together in long, intertwined strands that glue themselves to submerged objects and plants. Because breeding puddles can be short-lived, tadpoles must emerge from eggs and transform to adults quickly — sometimes in as little as two weeks.

The skin of Woodhouse's toads has the dual function of taking on water (through the rich capillary system on their bellies) and exuding a toxic mucus that repels most predators — but doesn't appear to lessen their popularity with hognose snakes.

Like most other members of the toad and frog order, Woodhouse's toads are voracious predators, eating virtually anything that moves and isn't too big to stuff into their mouths. Look for them hunting insects under lights.

Delicious Breath Unfresheners

As mountain folk have long known, wild leeks are good for warding off rheum, ague, chilblains, collywobbles, and, especially, neighbors — unless, as so frequently happens, all the neighbors are eating them at once. Breath fresheners they're not, but leeks — called "ramps" or "rampscallions" in the southern Appalachians, where whole towns turn out for ramp-gathering/eating festivals — are generally said to be the most delectable of all onions and garlics, wild or domestic. What's more, they're rich in vitamin C and have the same capacity for reducing cholesterol as garlic.

Striking green against the drab forest duff of early spring, these lovely, orchidlike members of the lily family abound in the deciduous woods of eastern North America.

Look for the flat, rubbery leaves in moist, shady areas. Any doubt about what you've found will be thoroughly erased by crushing a leaf and inhaling the strong onion odor. Leek leaves and, later, their bulbs are superb in scrambled eggs, mashed potatoes, soups, and casseroles or as onion substitutes in any recipe.

Uncommon Courtship

Common terns are now courting, especially on islands in northern temperate zones around the globe where gently sloping land embraces the sea and big lakes. Watch for their distinctive flight displays in which a male, shadowed by a female, flies along with a small fish in his bill. When she overtakes him, he'll drop his head, turn away, and hold his wings high over his back. At the same time she'll thrust her head forward and hold her wings down, then start a sharp downward glide, tilting from side to side.

On the ground a male may march in front of the female in a semicircle, lower his head, raise his head, bend forward, and kick back with his feet. Often he'll carry a small fish, presumably a signal of his intention to copulate. The female expresses interest — at least in the fish — by emitting a "ki-ki" call and hunching over. Sometimes another male will ape this behavior, thereby acquiring a free meal.

Also called sea swallows, these graceful, agile birds cover astonishing distances in migration. One individual, banded in Finland, was captured 16,000 miles away in Australia.

Down to the Crawdad Hole

People catch crawdads mainly to eat or to use for bait. But there's an even better reason — to admire them. The best time is early spring, when you're still beset with cabin fever and not yet distracted by things like warblers, garden plants, and lawns.

Crawdads (a.k.a. crayfish, crawfish, ditch bugs) are lobsters that moved up out of the estuaries, miniaturized, and evolved into mostly freshwater forms. About half the world's 500 species reside in North America. Turn over rocks in streams and ponds, and if you don't mind a gentle nip, grab the finger-size crustaceans before they snap their paddle tails and scoot away backward. Note the stalk-mounted eyes, the long, whiplike antennae, and the swimmerets along the abdomen — exquisite, featherlike organs with twin paddles joined at the tip.

At this season the swimmerets of some specimens may be covered with as many as 700 dark globules. They're eggs, attached by a waterproof glue called glair.

Hummer Pit Stops

Now, in our desert Southwest, spectacular foot-long clusters of red blooms hang from the branch ends of the cactuslike ocotillo, a.k.a. "devil's walking stick." And just in time, because flights of northbound hummingbirds, their main pollinators, are in desperate need of energy fixes. Few, if any, insects can reach the nectar, but carpenter bees — those excavators responsible for much of the damage to rafters, doors, siding, and sills blamed on ants and termites — "cheat" by cutting through the inch-long flowers.

A prime ocotillo may be close to 200 years old and have 100 spiny stems rising from its base. For this plant fall may come half a dozen times a year when dry spells cause it to shed its leaves. They grow back fast with a good rain.

In addition to sustaining hummingbirds, the ocotillo is an important food source for mule deer, white-tailed deer, bighorn sheep, and antelope ground squirrels. The Apache people used the powdered roots to treat wounds and the flowers to treat coughs. In frost-free parts of its range, ocotillo can be easily propagated by jamming cuttings into the ground.

Salt Seekers

Who's been eating the canoe paddles, the boat transoms, the truck tires, the work boots, the workbench, the out-house floor? If you live in or around a forest, there is one likely culprit: the orange-toothed, squint-eyed, nearsighted porcupine, alias quill pig. At this time of year, porcupines are leaving the rocky dens where they slept away the day-light hours of winter. They won't return until late fall — except to die. Now they crave salt, especially the females, who are losing sodium through the production of milk for the single pups. Virtually any item touched by human sweat or urine is greedily devoured, even glass.

Because their only serious enemies are fishers and cougars, porcupines are docile when confronted by humans. Press them, though, and they'll turn their raised backs toward you, protecting their heads against a tree or under their chests. The barbed, loosely attached quills, which the animals appear to "shoot" with swift swipes of their tails, are drawn into a victim's flesh by muscle action. They can kill by migrating to the heart or brain.

Sweet, Sticky Tree

Now coming into bloom in the eastern third of our nation is our tallest hardwood — the tulip tree, named for its spectacular orange-tinged, yellow-green flowers. Although it's also called yellow poplar, it's really a member of the magnolia family. There are but two species — one in the New World, one in the Old.

Because tulip trees can attain diameters of 12 feet and heights of 200 feet, they were used by Native Americans and early settlers to make dugout canoes. In 1799 Daniel Boone packed his belongings and family into a 60-foot tulip-tree canoe and struck off down the Ohio River to resettle in Spanish Missouri.

Few, if any, North American plants generate more nectar per bloom than tulip trees. Bees working a grove have produced as much as 100 pounds of harvestable honey per hive. Stand under the flowers and you can feel the steady rain of sticky nectar. Park under them and you'll need a car wash.

Griffins

If you think griffins — eagle-beaked lions capable of flight — are mythical, you aren't looking closely enough. In late spring, most anywhere in the United States where dirt or sand is warm and dry, ant lions are waiting at the bottom of conical pits, an inch or two across at the top, that they've excavated by inscribing concentric and ever-deeper rings. The ant lion's alternate name, "doodlebug," derives from the rambling, doodlelike patterns it leaves as it crawls around looking for the right place to dig.

It waits just under the point of the inverted cone, sometimes with its sicklelike mandibles showing. When an ant or small insect stumbles into the pit, the ant lion kicks up sand or dirt, causing miniature landslides and sending the victim tumbling to its doom. When you find a cone, tickle the sides with a pine needle and watch the puffs of material thrown into the air by the deluded ant lion.

Ant lions go dormant when disturbed, so they're easily caught with a spoon. Keep one in a jar full of sand, and feed it ants. Eventually it will pupate, then emerge as a laceywinged, sluggish flier resembling a damselfly save for its clubbed antennae.

Large-Finned House Dads

In clear, cool, rocky lakes and streams across the United States, smallmouth bass — actually a species of sunfish — are easing into shallows. The males, smaller than females, come first, cutting nests in gravel with their broad tails, then herding in their mates — often more than one. The male guards the eggs, fanning them with his tail, then broods the young. When males are on their nests they're extremely aggressive and will hit virtually any bait or lure, even after they have been caught and released the same day.

A smallmouth's mouth is small only in comparison with that of its bigger and more ubiquitous cousin — the largemouth bass of warmer water. With its oversize fins, an adaptation to moving water, the smallmouth might better be called "largefin bass." Before 1869 smallmouths were largely restricted to the Lake Ontario and Ohio River drainage systems. But toted in water tenders and tanks of the early railroads, they fanned out across the continent with their human admirers. Pound for pound, few, if any, freshwater fish are stronger. Today, thanks to the efforts of Ray Scott and the 600,000-member Bass Anglers Sportsman Society that he founded, most serious bass fishermen no longer kill their catch.

Matron of the Eaves

To be chosen by eastern phoebes means that you and your dwelling have not pressed too harshly on the living earth. Watch for these gray, bewhiskered flycatchers hovering near the edge of your roof or perched on a nearby branch, tails pumping as both sexes shout their raspy, incessant "feebee" or "feebeleee." Now, under the eaves, the female begins laying eggs in her nest of mud, moss, and grass — one each morning until there are four or five. You'll know the eggs have hatched when both parents flutter in and out of the nest every few minutes. Usually, they will raise another brood later in summer.

Fiddler on the Marsh

When mud and sand suck warmth from the high sun, the fiddle section rises and pirouettes across the fragrant marsh, silently accompanying the symphony of shorebirds, breaking waves, and sea wind through cordgrass. From southern California to Baja, along our Gulf Coast, around Florida, and north to New England, you'll encounter sundry species of fiddler crab, so named for the male's enlarged claw. On some marshes there may be 150,000 fiddlers to the acre.

When a courting male spies a female, he'll rear up and wave his fiddle higher and higher until he almost tips over. If she shows interest, he'll rush back and forth between her and the entrance to his burrow. Then he'll duck inside and drum on the walls with his big claw. When the female enters he'll guide her down to the mating chamber, then slip back and shut the entrance with a mud plug. The female incubates her eggs for a fortnight, then returns to the surface to send her brood off on the big flood tide of the new or full moon. They'll mature in the estuary for four weeks, then return as subadults under the next new or full moon.

How the West Got Gold

The California poppy has been widely transplanted around the nation, but only in its native range — California and thin slices of western Oregon, Washington, Nevada, and the Baja Peninsula — does it gild entire valleys and foothills to elevations of 7,000 feet. "To one who loves them in their glorious native hues, the white [cultivated] varieties seem almost repulsive," writes Timothy Coffee in *The History and Folklore of North American Wildflowers*. "Compare one of these small, pale flowers with the great, rich, orange ones that glorify some favored regions in the Mojave Desert, and we feel the enervating and decadent influence of civilization." When the first Spanish explorers beheld the massive, almost fluorescent spring blooms sweeping across rich alluvial soils, they called the land the "Golden West." In fact, legend has it that California's real gold was created by the falling petals.

The flowers close in late afternoon, providing snug refuge for insect pollinators that fly by day. California poppies do not stupefy in the fashion of Old-World opium poppies, but they contain a painkiller that Native Americans found useful for relieving toothaches.

Return of the Striper

Fresh from the chill Atlantic, silver fish clad in the black pinstripes of football referees (but blessed with better eyesight) are pouring into the Hudson, the Delaware, and the rivers of Chesapeake Bay to spawn in fresh water. The striped bass, a.k.a. "striper," is capable of attaining weights of more than 100 pounds. Ten to fifty males orbit the larger female, churning the surface and racing over her on their sides, as if wounded. A 4-pound female can produce 426,000 eggs; a 55-pounder, 4.2 million. Stripers, which range naturally from New Brunswick to Florida and west to Louisiana, have been introduced on the Pacific coast and in freshwater rivers and impoundments around the nation.

Recent fluctuations in the native Atlantic population illustrate what waggish conservationists have called "the First Maxim of Fisheries Management" — that is, we don't start managing a stock until we almost wipe it out. In the late 1970s Atlantic stripers crashed, due largely to overfishing, but in 1984 Congress relieved the states of management authority and awarded it to the feds. Today, after strict bag limits, the stock has rebounded. But according to the Atlantic States Marine Fisheries Commission, striped bass are being overfished.

Call from the Distant Past

Impoverished is the soul unstirred by the voice of the male bullfrog when first it breaks the silence of the May twilight. The deep, resonant "jug-o'-rum" — felt as much as heard — is a call from Earth's distant past, ages before the dinosaurs, when the first amphibians staggered out of Devonian seas to dominate the land for 70 million years.

The bullfrog occurs naturally in the eastern and central United States. Unfortunately, it has also been unleashed in our West and other nations, where it is trashing native ecosystems. The diet of this, our largest frog, consists of insects, fish, rodents, snakes, other frogs, birds — basically, any moving object it can stuff into its enormous mouth, often with its "hands." Wildlife photographer John Swedberg of Millbury, Massachusetts, once found a bullfrog that apparently had choked to death on an adult bluejay.

Most bullfrogs are green, but a few are yellow, white, or even sky blue. Don't look for them in vernal pools; their tadpoles take two or more years to transform and therefore need permanent water. Grab a bullfrog and it may scream as loud and long as the heroine of a 1950s horror movie.

Hated to Abundance

The music of song dogs, as coyotes are often called, can be heard almost anywhere in North America not permanently ice covered. But there's more of it now that pups are testing their independence and getting called back to their dens by nervous parents. Wrestling and playing tug-of-war with bones and scraps of skin, the pups will mat down wide swaths of meadow grass.

At this age learning to fear humans is a work in progress. Move slowly and you can get close to them, perhaps perceiving the species in a new light. Human hatred of coyotes and their main predators, gray wolves, has been responsible for the coyote's astonishing success. When we started exterminating wolves, coyotes expanded their range. When we finished with wolves and concentrated on "coyote control," coyotes expanded their range still farther, compensating for increased mortality by producing more pups.

Morphological differences are often dramatic among the 19 recognized subspecies. For example, the Mearns coyote of our western deserts rarely reaches 25 pounds, while the more wolflike northeastern coyote can reach 70 pounds.

In the West and Midwest coyotes and badgers commonly form hunting partnerships in which the badger digs out rodents and the coyote pounces on them. The badger will reject a coyote's invitation to romp, but it will allow it to lie down beside it and even make contact. The more demonstrative coyote expresses delight at the approach of a badger by wagging its tail and rolling on its back.

Hunted to Abundance

The only thing a tom turkey displaying on a spring strutting ground can possibly be mistaken for, say veteran wild turkey hunters, is a politician. The fleshy parts of his face turn bright red; he puffs himself up, spreads his tail, struts back

and forth, and spews rhetoric best translated as "gobble, gobble, gobble, gobble."

There are only two species of turkey: *Meleagris gallopavo* of North America (represented in the wild by five subspecies and domesticated by Native Americans about 2,000 years ago) and the smaller, more colorful *M. ocellata* of southern Mexico and Central America. Other species, now extinct, lived on both New World continents, but apparently turkeys have never occurred naturally anywhere else.

Nearly wiped out by market hunters, wild turkeys have been restored by intelligent hunting regulations and state trap-and-transfer programs funded by sportsmen. Since 1930 they've increased in North America from something like 20,000 to about five million.

Bunny Hop

In spring, as at any other time of year save fall in the North, an eastern cottontail rabbit's fancy turns to sex. But now, when succulent new growth lures eastern cottontail rabbits onto close-cropped grass most anywhere east of the Rockies, you have the best chance of witnessing their courtship dance. As fireflies wink and caroling thrushes usher in the twilight, take a seat 100 feet from where you have recently seen "bunny buttons," the cottontail's round, sometimes wrinkled droppings. (Those produced by deer are elongated and smooth.)

There is no predicting what the dancers will do. Sometimes they will race over the grass, inscribing loops and circles and leaping high into the air. Or they may bound over each other in wild games of leapfrog, kicking at the sky. Suddenly, they will dash into cover and just as suddenly burst forth again. A female may rise up on her hind legs and punch the smaller male with her forefeet as he races by, or she may jump into the air and spray him with urine as he passes underneath.

Ground-foraging birds such as flickers and robins are remarkably tolerant of these antics, merely fluttering several feet into the air to avoid getting run over, then settling back to work.

Desert Starbursts

The deserts of northern Mexico and the southwestern United States hoard their beauty for months, then emit it in bursts as bright and brief as meteors. One magic night in June, desert shrubs and trees will suddenly be hung with fallen stars five inches across and still glowing. They are the white, silky blossoms of the night-blooming cereus, known in Spanish as *reina de la noche*, or queen of the night.

This otherwise inconspicuous, finger-thin cactus needs the supporting embrace of a "nurse plant" such as creosote bush or mesquite so that it may grow high enough to lure night-tripping pollinators, notably sphinx moths. To efficiently attract these insects, most plants unfurl their

blossoms at the same time. The scene is something out of *A Midsummer Night's Dream* — big moths hovering in a blur of wingbeats, dipping into moonlit flowers, then buzzing into the night. At first light the flowers vanish for another year.

Spying on Foxes

It's a major challenge to find a place in North America without red foxes, the most widespread terrestrial carnivore on Earth. And you don't have to leave suburbia to find their dens. Look for a mound of dirt and a burrow on a wooded slope. If it's a fox den, the entrance is likely to be lined with bones and feathers and such playthings as shoes, gloves, shotgun shells, and plastic trucks.

In May the plump, fuzzy pups begin to venture outside the den. They are not yet afraid of humans. No harm to sit for an hour and snap photos as they loll in the sun, play tug-of-war with their toys, or wrestle with each other, turning somersaults. A pup may even waddle over and sniff you.

One reason for the astonishing success of this species is that it will eat almost anything — carrion, small mammals, turtles, frogs, fish, birds, eggs, insects, worms, fruit, nuts, grain. A red fox will pick berries with great delicacy one at a time, puckering its lips.

Cuckoo Come Lately

In late spring, when almost all other birds are incubating eggs or feeding hatchlings, yellow-billed cuckoos breeze in from Central and South America to set up housekeeping in old orchards, thickets, and shrublands in the eastern United States and isolated locales in the West. It's a hurried job, sometimes taking as little as 17 days from egg laying to fledging. One day the quill-covered nestlings look like porcupines, and flight seems out of the question. The next day feathers burst forth from their sheathes, and the birds take to the air. Occasionally, the process is so rushed that nest building is skipped and the female drops her eggs in another bird's clutch. Usually, though, the surrogate parents are other yellow-billed cuckoos, and such behavior may be less Old-World-cuckoo-style nest parasitism than "brood cooperative," duck-style egg dumping.

Yellow-billed cuckoos eat fruit and all manner of insects, including hairy caterpillars that repulse other birds.

They are among the very few North American birds capable of preying on gypsy-moth larvae; and when their stomachs get so perforated with spines that digestion is impaired, they merely regurgitate the linings and grow new ones — "a process," noted early-twentieth-century ornithologist Edward Forbush, "that would be beneficial to some unfeathered bipeds could they compass it."

Winged Goblins

Burrowing owls perform all sorts of functions useful to humans, none more so than demonstrating to infertile minds that goblins really do exist. On prairies, grasslands, and open areas in southwest Canada, the western states, Florida (which sustains an isolated and rapidly dwindling population), and from Mexico to southern Argentina, these small, scowling, long-legged owls can be seen at any time of day standing beside burrows abandoned by ground dwellers, sometimes bobbing their heads and cackling demonically. During spring courtship a pair will stand atop their appropriated burrow, stretch their legs and wings, preen, and nibble each other, and alternately hover 20 feet in the air, appearing utterly unbirdlike — otherworldly, in fact.

Perhaps to conceal their odor from predators, burrowing owls frequently line their subterranean nests with cow chips. Come too close, and they'll emit a superb imitation of an angry prairie rattlesnake.

Moon Flakes

Nothing imparts more magic to a late-spring evening than the appearance of a luna moth. Perhaps it clings to your porch screen or dances fairylike around a streetlamp; or maybe you catch its shadow as it flutters across the bright face of its namesake, long tails tossing in unstable, seemingly impossible flight.

Many insect guides report that these five-inch-wide moon flakes are fading from the American scene, rare to the point of endangerment. But recently we've come to understand that throughout most of their range, from the East Coast to the Dakotas and Texas, luna moths are actually common. It's just that they are rarely seen because adults live only for about a week. As with other giant silk moths, their digestive tracts have disintegrated during pupation so they don't eat. Basically, they're flying gametes. When darkness settles, the female releases a pheromone detected at great distances by the male's antennae, more feathery than the female's.

Females deposit eggs on such plants as walnut, butternut, sweetgum, paper birch, persimmon, alder, beech, and willow. Find one of the light-green, dark-headed, yellow-striped larvae on any of these host plants, and enclose it with netting to protect it from predators. Make sure to leave plenty of space for it to feed. The following spring check the cocoon regularly.

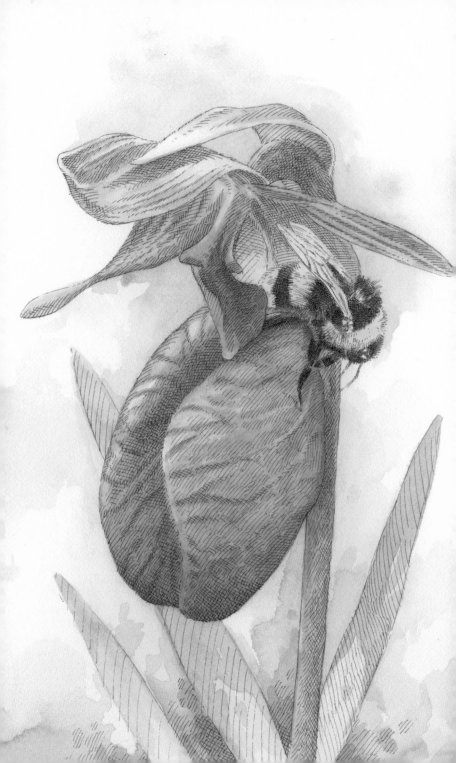

Summer

Summer is a season when nature slows down and draws her breath. Most birds have gotten where they were going and fledged their young. Most fish have finished spawning and are actively feeding again. Most reptiles and amphibians have laid their eggs and returned to their normal haunts. Most mammals have recovered from the weight loss of winter and the stress of mating.

But for some species, summer can be a test. During droughts insectivorous birds — especially hatchlings — may starve. Brook trout, the descendants of oceangoing char landlocked by ancient glaciers, huddle in dwindling pools of spring water, shaded only by tangles of jewelweed and cut off from the rest of the stream by sandbars that blaze scarlet with blooming cardinal flowers.

In Atlantic and Pacific drainages, adult salmon hold below dams and rapids, waiting for the spates that will let them climb to their natal tributaries. Most denizens of arid and desert environments hole up or bury themselves by day to escape the heat.

Some creatures don't have the luxury of waiting until fall to migrate. Broadwing hawks, for example, spiral up on thermals in "kettles" of a hundred or more, then glide for miles, gradually losing altitude until they hit more thermals. Nighthawks — not raptors but goatsuckers related to whip-poor-wills — may form and depart before the end of August. Hummingbirds, flycatchers, storm petrels, piping plovers, warbling vireos, Louisiana waterthrushes, blue-winged warblers, and solitary sandpipers may precede them or follow in a matter of days. Monarch butterflies — stately fliers that conserve energy with slow, strong wingbeats and long glides — stage on trees along both coasts. You may encounter them now when you're far out at sea and they are on their way to Mexico.

In high summer still air hanging over still water is patrolled by flights of damselflies — blue and brown, some in tandem. Higher up, dragonflies hawk gnats and are themselves hawked by kingbirds that dash out from dead branches, flutter and twist, and settle back with their meals. In the woods the damselflies called ebony jewelwings flutter over parched brooks and seeps or perch in iridescent, green-black clusters on brush, sedges, and the drooping seed heads of grass. In meadows milkweed pods unzip, and their silk billows up on the warm wind. In wetlands and along the vegetated borders of ponds and rivers, the carapaces of basking turtles glisten from logs and rocks. As vernal pools dry up, newly matured salamanders head for the uplands, while encysted embryos of fairy shrimp settle into salty leaf litter, where, later, they will (indeed must) dry and freeze.

Summer is a quieter time than spring, yet it is far from silent. Birdsong diminishes, but now there are new carolers. High overhead, etched on azure, goldfinches dip and bob and shout "perchickory." They have waited for ripe thistles, then used the silk for nesting material and the seeds for nourishment. All day, from high in the forest canopy, red-eyed vireos chant, "Here am I; where are you?" In the heat of midmorning, cicadas buzz from hardwood groves; gray tree frogs trill from brush on still afternoons; bullfrogs boom at night from swamps and shores. As the evenings grow cooler, katydids start, then crickets.

Almost everywhere in our nation, summer seems to smell better than other seasons. My favorite fragrances are those of new-mown hay, rose hips, tidal marsh, dried kelp on granite, sun on old creosoted planks, pond water that's bathtub warm and blooming with clean native algae. And best of all, the sweet pepperbush — a.k.a. summer sweet — that perfumes the lakeside breeze, intoxicates butterflies and bees, and for almost three weeks seems to halt Earth in its orbit.

Enjoy the silent, luminous showers (the Perseid meteors that streak from the constellation Perseus on midsummer nights, usually peaking on August 12) and the loud, cooling deluge after alplike cumulonimbus clouds, slashed by lightning, have blotted out the bloated sun. Don't miss the chance to go berrying. Blackberries, raspberries, blueberries, huckleberries, and wild grapes are sweet and ripe, but get after them promptly because they dry out fast or are eaten by birds and insects. Punch holes in a large coffee can and hang it around your neck so you can pick with both hands. With their tartness blueberries make the best muffins. But huckleberries are sweeter on cereal even if they do have seeds that get stuck between your teeth. Nothing is better on bagels or toast than wild-grape jam.

If you find your spirits ebbing with the brightening of hardwood leaves and the shortening of precious days, be of good cheer. Remember that the end-of-summer blues are a vestigial malady, a conditioned reflex from that time when fun and freedom abruptly ended and you were dragged out of woods and water and away from fish, frogs, turtles, dogs, and other friends to be incarcerated in school for nine months. For adults, at least, there is no loss of freedom when summer ends. In fact, when the crowds disperse, there's a net gain.

A Vision for Thieves

In most of North America, there is a delicious interface
between spring and summer, when those who have been
waiting repair quietly to secret places to pick blueberries
with beak, muzzle, and fingers. Some blueberry species
grow high, some grow low, and all favor forest disturbances
such as burns and blowdowns. As Robert Frost, who reveled
in transitions such as blueberry time, noted:

> *But get the pine out of the way, you may burn*
> *The pasture all over until not a fern*
> *Or grass-blade is left, not to mention a stick,*
> *And presto, they're up all around you as thick*
> *And hard to explain as a conjuror's trick.*

On those fleeting mornings when ripe fruit and dew
hang together like sapphires and diamonds, there for the
thieving, don't miss the chance to take children blueberry-
ing. Note the color of their tongues when they tell you all
the berries went into the pail.

Plumed Hunters

The best tonic for those benighted souls who imagine
that the fight to save wildlife is hopeless is to watch great
egrets — the backs of both sexes resplendent with long
breeding plumes — stalk across newly thawed marsh and
tidal flat. Unlike some other members of the heron family,

they hunt only by day. Suddenly, one will freeze — maybe for 10 minutes — then harpoon a fiddler crab or killifish. Among our herons only the great blue — also white on occasion but lacking the great egret's black legs — is larger.

Today, from Oregon to Massachusetts and south, the great egret is the most abundant white heron near water, but a century ago we almost lost it. Perhaps we would have if it hadn't been for the Audubon Society, which offered public lectures on such topics as "Woman as a Bird Enemy," and activists such as Celia Thaxter, a noted poet of the day, who published vitriolic attacks on women adorned with egret plumes. "It was merely a waste of breath," she wrote after she'd lectured one slave of fashion barely visible under an enormous hat, "and she went her way, a charnel house of beaks and claws and bones and feathers and glass eyes upon her fatuous head."

Loud Acrobats

It is a warm June night, and an eyed elater — a creature that looks as frightening as its name sounds — is on your well-lighted porch, trying to enter your house. Abundant in the East and as far west as Texas and South Dakota, this is one of our largest click beetles, approaching two inches in length. It derives its name from the two black, white-rimmed "snake-eye" spots on the upper part of its thorax, apparently an adaptation to frighten predators. So what should you do: retreat to the cellar, fetch a broom, or rise and tickle the intruder? Take the last course of action because it will elicit a fascinating show. First, your eyed elater is apt to play dead. Persist in your tickling and it will emit a loud click, springing as high as six inches into the air. The response will startle you even if you're expecting it, so you can imagine how it would affect, say, a foraging skunk. There's another good reason to welcome eyed elaters. Their larvae, "wireworms," don't damage crops like the wireworms of many other click-beetle species; instead they prey on such insect pests as wood borers and flies.

Leopard in the Grass

In early summer, these leopards are stalking prey through the high grass of southern meadows. But in the North you can still hear them roaring (or, perhaps more descriptively, "snoring") from the surface — and even below the surface — of ponds and dawdling streams. These leopards are semiterrestrial frogs that inhabit most of temperate North America, save the West Coast. Taxonomists argue about how many subspecies of leopard frogs there are but generally agree on four species — northern, southern, plains, and Rio Grande.

Watch for leopards as they hunt crickets, grasshoppers, spiders, and such. You can even feed them by hitching a thread to a long stick, tying on a large insect or a piece of fish or meat, and making it hop along the ground. They'll snap it up, then stuff it into their mouths with their "hands."

Catching leopard frogs with your hands is a challenge because of their rapid, zigzag leaps, but if you succeed, you'll discover that they "chuckle" only when annoyed.

Once the most widely distributed frogs in North America, leopards are experiencing a drastic decline. Among the many causes is their widespread collection by supply houses for classroom study.

Painted Ladies

Gaudy as confetti, painted lady butterflies waft north or south, depending on hemisphere, following the wave of new bloom. After the drabness of winter and mud time, these vast migrations would be tonic enough, but for those dispirited by the plights of specialized species, they provide a different, much-needed perspective. How refreshing to contemplate a lovely creature thriving all over the world — not because it was superimposed on native ecosystems or because humans have destroyed its competitors, but because it is adapted to virtually every moderately open tropical, temperate, and subarctic landscape on every continent save Australia and Antarctica. So widespread is this, perhaps Earth's least endangered butterfly, that an alternate name for it is the cosmopolitan.

Unlike the migration of monarchs, the migration of painted ladies is mostly one way — poleward from sunny wintering grounds where, also unlike monarchs, they hibernate. When you see a painted lady, or lots of them, don't just admire; think about the species and its statement of hope.

Flying Cows

As the Atlantic warms, vast schools of cow-nosed rays, some of the females weighing as much as 35 pounds, waft northward from Brazil, entering bays all the way to Massachusetts to feast on bivalves. They excavate their prey by fanning sand and sediment with their broad wings and simultaneously sucking it into their mouths and blowing it out their gill slits. A school thus engaged will muddy a large area; and, because they stir up other organisms, they're frequently attended by such fish as striped bass and cobia.

The cow-nosed ray is armed with a venomous tail spike, as Captain John Smith learned in 1608 when he stabbed one with his sword near the Rappahannock River. The ray stabbed back with a very palpable hit to Smith's shoulder, causing such intense pain that his crew dug a grave for him. By evening, however, Smith had improved enough to eat the ray for his supper. The scene of this duel is still known as Stingray Point.

Mega-Tern

Watch that pair of terns more closely. They are not as near as you supposed; they're just huge — the largest terns in the world, in fact. Nor are these herring-gull-size birds mated. The one with more dark spots on its wings is following the other. The leader, croaking like a raven with a cold, is the parent. The youngster, emitting a thin, pathetic wail, is begging to be fed, though with scant success at this time of year.

The Caspian tern, one of the few birds that accompany their offspring on migration, breeds at the edge of the world's temperate and subtropical seas, as well as at many large inland lakes. In Labrador, John James Audubon observed Caspian terns driving off nest predators such as the powerful pomarine jaeger.

Reptile Calisthenics

As the sun lingers over the northern hemisphere, fence lizards, a bit longer than a pencil, start breeding throughout the southern two-thirds of our nation. When trying to attract mates, the males appear to do push-ups, displaying patches of iridescent blue on belly and throat. Look for these quick, dark sprites in almost any habitat — open woodlands, grassy dunes, and prairies, but not deserts. A fence lizard can be closely observed or photographed on a tree, but you'll need the help of a friend. Send him or her around the trunk, and like a squirrel, your subject will ease around to your side.

Barren-Land Bounder

Under the more arid regions of our Southwest, in dens lined with plant material, kangaroo rats are giving birth, usually to two to four young. The animals you see now, almost always at night, are likely to be males. There are 22 species, many of them threatened or endangered because so much of their habitat has been developed or tilled. Like their namesakes, kangaroo rats propel themselves with well-developed hind legs, balancing with long tails. In some species the tails are longer than the bodies, and by swinging them the animals can change directions in midleap.

As they exhale, kangaroo rats are able to recover water vapor through their nasal passages, and they can metabolize the water they need from seeds. So powerful are their kidneys that they require only a quarter of the water used by humans to excrete the same amount of urea.

Turtle Nests

The glowing yellow undershell, the splashes of scarlet on neck and carapace, the yellow stripes on head and eye — it all seems too much, as if some grade-school artist had gone wild with high-gloss enamels. Two months ago, while frogs still slept, North America's four races of painted turtle — probably our most abundant, widespread, and beloved freshwater reptile — began to mate, males swimming

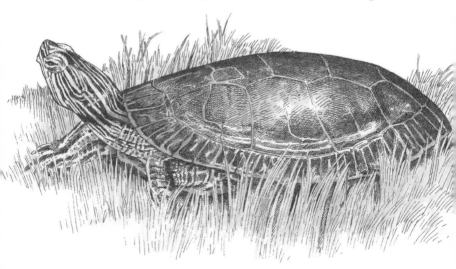

backward ahead of the females and tickling them in the face with their long foreclaws, then dropping with them to copulate on the muddy bottom.

In May and on into high summer, look for females on their way to sunny, sandy nesting sites. Follow one, taking care not to get too close, and watch as she plants her front feet, then digs a four-inch hole with her hind legs. She'll deposit as many as 20 eggs, then cover them. As with other reptiles, the sex of the developing embryos is determined by temperature. The cooler the nest, the more males; the warmer, the more females. Hatchlings usually overwinter in the nest, emerging the next spring in perfect health, despite the freezing of more than half their body fluids.

Whistler's Father

If you live in the eastern two-thirds of the nation and south of the northern tier, don't miss the predawn concert of the male bobwhite quail. It starts in brushy grasslands or in the understory of open woods with the first red wash on the eastern sky — a whistling so loud and clear that obedient dogs have responded to it: "White. Bob White."

Unlike most gallinaceous birds, the male helps with nest building, incubating eggs, and rearing young. The great ornithologist Arthur Cleveland Bent recalled how a bobwhite performed a variant rendition of the "broken-wing act" by flying at him and, with a shrill whistle, collapsing at his feet as if it were dead: "I stooped and put my hand

upon his extended wings and could easily have caught him. The young birds, at the cry of the parent, flew in all directions; and their devoted father soon followed them, and began calling them in a low cluck, like the cry of a brown thrasher."

For protection, quail will arrange themselves in a circle, facing outward like musk oxen, but instead of attacking approaching predators, they'll flush together in an explosion of wings.

Artist in the Garden

Her tapestry is best displayed in early summer when plants are high. The garden spider starts at about four in the morning, anchoring lines to surrounding vegetation, spinning a bicycle-wheel pattern, then connecting the spokes with strands that spiral toward the center. For thread she uses a substance called fibroin, which has a tensile strength greater than steel and a stretchability twice that of nylon. On each of roughly 1,300 strands she applies liquid adhesive in evenly spaced droplets. When rain or wind tears the web, she recycles the fibroin by eating it and using the protein to generate more.

When first you see the orb web of the garden spider, it is apt to be strung with beads of dew that flash in the morning sun. If you find yourself wondering how anything that beautiful could issue from anything that ugly, keep looking. Maybe you'll come to agree with E. B. White's Charlotte, who declared, "Almost all spiders are rather nice-looking." You might even decide that the garden spider, colored as brightly as any goldfinch, is as beautiful as her creation.

Pruned Pioneer

You'll encounter them all year, but they're especially active in summer. Waddling through your headlight beams, they look like rats, only bigger, fatter, toothier, and slower. Opossums invaded North America from the south about the time Caucasians invaded it from the east, and both invasions are still in progress. Because opossums evolved in a mild climate, the ones in the snowbelt from Yankeeland to Colorado are apt to have frost-pruned ears and tails. The loss of ear tissue only makes the beasts look uglier (if possible), but because they store a lot of fat in their tails, the abbreviation of those appendages may curtail their northward expansion.

The opossum is the continent's only marsupial. Females deliver bee-size young after only 12½ days of gestation. Newborns, essentially mobile embryos, haul themselves up into a kangaroo-style pouch, where they either die or find a nipple that expands in their mouths, buttoning them into place. In one study, a researcher could fit only 21 beans into the brainpan of an opossum skull but needed 150 to fill the brainpan of a raccoon. The opossum's remarkable success proves what countless mid- and low-level business managers already know — that intelligence is no criterion for advancement.

Bumblebee Traps

In most of eastern North America, dark pine-oak woods are bright with pink lady's slippers, one of our largest and most spectacular orchids. In the northern part of their range they tend to be white. North American Indians, who adorned their hair with the blossoms, called them moccasin flowers.

The plant sends forth two long leaves from the base of the stalk at the same time it blooms. Petals are joined together in a single red-veined, walnut-size sac with a fissure down the front — a one-way entrance for pollinators. As the pollinator, usually a medium-size bumblebee, crawls out either of two escape holes at the top, its pollen-covered

back brushes the female part of the plant. As it exits, a small green projection dusts its back with pollen for the female part of the plant it will next visit. Touch one of these projections and note the gummy pollen on your finger.

Attack of the June Bugs

June bugs — those fearsome-looking scarab beetles that bang noisily against screens on warm spring and summer evenings — are much prized by children, who find them useful for frightening adults. June-bug phobia is a centuries-old tradition in the New World. As writer Sarah Orne Jewett noted in 1872: "Your life is made so wretched by their whizzing past your ears and dropping upon your table, not to speak of the horrible fear of their entangling themselves in your hair. . . . We ought to sympathize more tenderly with our young-lady friends who spend long seasons of dejection on the hall stairs because two or three energetic June Beetles have happened to come into the parlor to spend a social evening."

June bugs appear to seek entry to houses because they are attracted to light, and they bang because flying mobility has been sacrificed for protection by a second set of hard wings that are extended to the sides in flight. Like all proper monsters, most of the 200 or so species distributed throughout North America emerge from the earth at night. All are harmless. But the fat, white larvae of about 25 species feed on the roots of grass and, in large concentrations, can damage your lawn.

Beaks by Barnum & Bailey

When kelp-maned granite sheds its frozen crust, Atlantic puffins pause from their ocean wanderings. From Labrador to Maine and from Greenland and northern Russia to the Brittany coast, these cousins of the extinct great auk march stiffly onto rocky islands. The massive parrotlike beaks of both sexes glow with impossible shades and sequences of blue, orange, and yellow. In 1925 ornithologist Edward Howe Forbush described the puffin as "a solemnly comical Mr. Punch among birds" that speaks in "deep, sepulchral tones full of the deepest feeling and capable of harsh croakings."

Puffins emerge from the sea with fish draped neatly from their beaks like socks from a clothesline. It seems as if human fingers had to have helped with the arrangement, but the bird's raspy tongue holds each fish against spines on its palate so it can open its beak and grab another. In flight, puffins resemble badly thrown footballs; when they hit the water they keep "flying," propelled by short, powerful wings to depths of at least 80 feet.

Puffins are less popular as human fare now than in the days when it was believed that, because of their capacity for underwater flight, they were a cross between bird and fish and therefore could be eaten on Fridays without incurring the wrath of the Catholic Church.

Frogs That Change Color

What bird is that, calling from the high brush along the wet meadow in the heat of the summer twilight? A short trill, loud and resonant for one to three seconds, almost like the call of a red-bellied woodpecker. It's not a bird; it's a gray tree frog — found from New Brunswick to Florida and west to North Dakota and central Texas. Unlike good children, male gray tree frogs are more often heard than seen, because they sing from high perches and change color like a chameleon.

Gray tree frogs are fat and about two inches long. Depending on their surroundings, their color may vary from gray to brown to green to pearl gray to white. Use a flashlight to locate the singer. Don't give up. Eventually you'll spot him, clutching a branch with his suction-cup toes, his throat ballooning like bubble gum.

Model for the Devout

Praying mantises, now approaching adulthood in field and garden, were placed on Earth to teach humankind the correct posture for addressing the Almighty — or so it has been reported by religious authorities. Although researchers have yet to prove this theory, what they have documented is no less astonishing. For example, the nearly six-inch-long Chinese mantis — introduced to this continent in the late 1800s and the largest and most widely distributed of our 20 species — will attack hummingbirds, frogs, and lizards. The European mantis — also an alien and pretty much restricted to the East — sometimes acquires two meals for the cost of one by seeking out the burrow of a ground wasp and waiting in ambush for the returning insect, which frequently comes in carrying prey for its young.

Mantises are among the few insects that can swivel their heads. This talent allows a female to respond to an amorous male, stealthily approaching her from behind, by literally biting his head off, an admonishment that impairs his sexual performance not a whit. This behavior, however, is rare and possibly unnatural; researchers have suggested that it is induced by distracting lab lights and insufficient feeding of study specimens.

Ghost Flowers

In the wet shade of the deep woods hide the ghost flowers of high summer. Throughout most of the United States and southern Canada, they stand in a clump with bowed heads, white and waxen, a vision from *Fantasia*. Note the raised nodules along the stalks. They're vestigial leaves, no longer needed by the Indian pipe because, unlike plants outside its tiny genus, it has no chlorophyll. Instead of manufacturing its food with nutrients and the energy of sunlight, the Indian pipe apparently steals it from fungi in the soil. Pick a flower, and it will turn black. Native Americans, from whose peace pipes the flower derives its name, mixed it with water and applied it to their eyes as a salve. For this reason the plant is also known as eyebright.

Matron of the Marsh

Hold on. Before you wander out to inspect that curious seven-foot-wide, three-foot-high mound of vegetation in the marsh, remember that — if you live anywhere from the coastal plain of North Carolina south to the Florida Keys and west to central Texas — you might be approaching the nest of an American alligator. That is not a great idea, because the female, who has just built the nest by cutting plants with her jaws and tail, guards it jealously. When she hears the hatchlings calling to her from inside, she'll dig them out.

The nest is usually constructed near a hole that the gator digs in the bank for rest and shelter. Such alligator wallows provide habitat for aquatic life and drinking water for terrestrial life during droughts. International traffic in alligator hide drastically reduced the species in the 1960s, but with federal protection, starting in 1970, alligators have recovered to the point that in many areas they're now nuisances.

Mini Pike

Take a closer look at those fish you thought were baby pickerel, pike, or muskellunge as they scoot or thrash — or hang, as if from mobiles — in sluggish streams, swamps, pond margins, and even floodwater. All pike spawn in early spring, but what are these hot-dog-size fish doing tearing up the shallows in large groups, broadcasting eggs and milt on thick vegetation?

They're adults, too — "little pickerel," as the two subspecies are collectively called. So closely are they related that they'll interbreed where ranges overlap. The grass pickerel, of the Mississippi and Gulf Coast drainages, lacks the crimson fins of the redfin pickerel, which is confined to waters collected by the Atlantic. Little pickerel have dark, tear-shaped markings under their eyes and blunter snouts than their larger cousins. In some areas they are being depressed by nonnative pike and bass unleashed on their habitat by an angling culture for which size and quality are synonyms.

Dinosaurs' Elder

When swamp and lakeshore flush with ripeness, there's a stirring in surrounding sandy soil. From the hills of Colorado to the salt marshes of the Atlantic and from Nova Scotia south to Ecuador, ancient beasts, older even than the dinosaurs, are cutting their way out of

Ping-Pong-ball-shaped eggs with their soon-to-be-shed egg teeth. Some of the hatchlings will stay in the earth until the following spring, but most will claw their way up into the sunlight. Then, through some unknown navigation system, they will strike out toward rivers, ponds, and swamps maybe half a mile away. There, over the course of perhaps a century, a few may grow to more than 70 pounds.

You can spend a lifetime in the outdoors and never encounter common snapping turtles emerging from their nest, but along roads, on dikes, and in dry meadows, it's not difficult to find the oval, eggshell-littered holes where nests have been. Dig around gently and you may find hatchlings that have died or haven't left. Adult snappers, which can't withdraw completely into their shells like other turtles, have evolved an aggressive response to potential predators. They will nail you if you mess with them on land, but when submerged they almost never bite a human.

Pulsating Parachutes

On bright, still summer afternoons you can see them blooming in lakes and sluggish river systems in at least 39 states — pulsating parachutes the size of dimes and quarters. These animals, at least as strange as any described in mythology or science fiction, are freshwater jellyfish — the free-swimming "medusa" stage of a tiny beast called a polyp that anchors itself to submerged plants and rocks. The circular edge of each medusa is ringed with 50 to 500 tentacles, each with thousands of stingers incapable of penetrating human skin but deadly to zooplankton. Fish will ingest medusae, but they quickly spit them out and sometimes dash around, obviously in discomfort. Crayfish are the only creatures known to eat them.

The stalklike polyps, which live in colonies, reproduce asexually by forming three radically different buds. One develops into another polyp and remains attached to the original; another develops into a cylindrical larva and crawls away to form a new polyp; and the third sheds medusae that can reproduce sexually, their eggs hatching into larvae that settle to the bottom and develop into polyps. In all but three known U.S. populations, however, medusae are either all male or all female. Apparently, our single species of polyp arrived from China (where there are four), stowing away on aquatic plants.

Raining Toads

A hard summer rain strews toads across the deserts and dry grasslands of our Southwest as if they had fallen from the firmament. Where no amphibian has walked for perhaps a year, the newly wet earth is suddenly alive with Couch's spadefoot toads — green or yellow, bug-eyed, and bleating from puddles like lambs separated from their ewes. Breeding and maturation of young must happen swiftly, because the puddles won't last. Eggs can hatch in 24 hours; tadpoles may develop into toads in nine days.

Keratinous "spades" on hind feet allow adults to dig three feet into the soil. Here, with metabolisms turned down to flickering pilot flames, they'll remain until the soil is again soaked.

Flying Lanterns

Few creatures are more stimulating to what Rachel Carson called our "sense of wonder" than the roughly 136 beetles of the family Lampyridae, which flash over North American meadows and gardens on soft spring and summer evenings. We know them as fireflies, or lightning bugs.

Each species has a pattern of flashes so distinctive as to be recognizable to attentive humans. Females lure males by answering their flashes, but females of some species mimic the flash sequences of others, luring males not as mates but as meals. Humans use the chemicals involved in the reaction to study diseases, including cancers.

For reasons not well understood, fireflies are in decline in much of the nation.

The poet David McCord, after explaining that real stars *"are all so far away for creature kind that hide by day,"* aptly described fireflies as *"little lanterns sailing by, / Like stars across a mimic sky, / Just high enough — but not too high."* Children should be sent

after them early and often. Never will they forget coursing through high grass with a net, sweeping lanterns from that mimic sky.

Great Expectorations

Who spat all over the meadow as if it were the dirt around home plate? Sometimes the frothy spittle hanging from the high grass is so profuse that farmers have trouble curing hay. The culprits are not ill-mannered ballplayers but larval froghoppers — relatives of cicadas and so named because of the adult's angular head, prominent eyes, and impressive leaping ability. Admonish a spittlebug (as the larva is called) to "keep the spit in your head" and it will comply, because everything comes out the other end — as much as 300 times its own weight in sap a day.

Unlike the sweet phloem sap savored by so many other creatures, the xylem sap sucked by the spittlebug is only 0.005 percent sugar, so the insect must pump furiously to gain more nutrients than it burns. As the sap passes through its digestive tract, a waxy bubble-making substance is added. On exiting the anus, it falls around the downward-facing larva, keeping it moist and discouraging predators. Gently part the foam with a grass stem and you'll see the green, plump, dark-eyed expectorator at work.

Summer Song

Now, in the heat of summer, the bird chorus has fallen silent. But in mixed or deciduous woodlands throughout the United States (save the extreme West and Southwest), one diminutive caroler perseveres. From high in the canopy the male red-eyed vireo chants his monotonous, robinlike refrain, with no respite at midday or even while foraging for caterpillars. Sometimes he's called preacher bird, because he punctuates the end of each phrase with a rising inflection as he chants, "You see it. You know it. Do you hear me? Do you believe it?"

Because the bird is something of a ventriloquist, vireo nests are often easier to spot than vireos. The nests are rare works of art, made with strips of birch bark, spider or caterpillar webbing, filaments from weed stems, paper from wasp nests, and egg cases of spiders. But just admire; collecting one, even after it has been abandoned, is a violation of the Migratory Bird Treaty Act.

Summer Snow

From British Columbia to Alberta and south to California and Wyoming, moist, forested mountains and foothills are draped in a new blanket of white. It consists of the profuse, saucer-shaped blooms of beargrass that tend to appear in five- to seven-year cycles and in large clumps atop stalks that may be six feet high. While the plant resembles bunchgrass, it's actually a perennial herb related to lilies. Extremely frost tolerant, it remains green through harsh northern winters.

The name "beargrass" may derive from the strong, bearlike odor of its blossoms or the fact that grizzlies use it to line their winter dens. Because it is relished by elk it is also called "elk grass." Other names include "fire lily" (it's usually the first plant to sprout from tough rhizomes in the wake of moderate forest fires) and "Indian basket" (western tribes wove its leaves into baskets, clothes, cooking pots, and even watertight vessels). Look for beargrass in cool forests of spruce, fir, larch, and whitebark pine.

Submersible Songbird

John Muir called it "the mountain stream's own darling, the hummingbird of blooming waters, loving rocky ripple-slopes and sheets of foam." In summer the robin-size American dipper — so named because, when perched, it dips up and down about 40 times a minute — hunts insect larvae in headwater streams of western high country, from Alaska to Panama. Gripping the smooth gravel with its feet, it walks to the water's edge and continues until it is well below the surface, easily negotiating currents that would sweep away a fisherman in chest waders. Beneath the flow, tiny flaps seal off nostrils, while a second, transparent set of eyelids serves as goggles.

Like the water nymphs of ancient lore, dippers sometimes dwell behind cataracts where the only access is through the falling water and where spray continually soaks their nests. Their call — a loud clicking, as if two stones were being struck together — evolved to make it clearly audible over the rushing water.

Pretty Peas

Now in the eastern two-thirds of our nation partridge peas, slender wildflowers two or three feet high, are in spectacular yellow bloom. Touch one of the leaves and, when it curls, you'll understand why the species is also called sensitive plant.

In some locations the flowers are already being replaced by flat 1½- to 2½-inch seedpods. Later, they will spiral open and shoot out seeds relished by all manner of wildlife, especially such partridgelike birds as bobwhite quail, ring-necked pheasants, and prairie chickens. The plant tissue itself is a larval food source for caterpillars of butterflies like the gray hairstreak, cloudless sulphur, sleepy orange, little yellow, and ceraunus blue. And the nectar — produced by the leaves, not blooms — nourishes bees and adult butterflies.

Rapid colonizers of disturbed land, partridge peas are useful in combating erosion. What's more, they fix nitrogen in the soil, thereby enriching it for other vegetation. Seeds can be collected in October and planted in late winter to late spring.

The Buzz on Cicadas

Any morning now you'll hear the song of high summer. When the July sun heats the earth to 80 degrees Fahrenheit, there's a rattle that progresses quickly to a rising buzz, beginning in one hardwood tree and — when a second percussionist picks it up — finishing in another. This haunting pitch issues from drum tissue stretched over the thorax of the male annual cicada or "harvestfly." "Locust" is another popular name, but a true locust is a type of grasshopper, while cicadas are related to leafhoppers.

Annual cicadas, of which there are about 70 species, occur most everywhere in the United States save its northwest corner. The dark, translucent-winged adults, two-thirds the length of the average human thumb and just as thick, live only about two weeks. Females lay their eggs in slits they cut in branches. Nymphs fall to the ground, burrowing quickly to the roots, where they subsist on sap, usually for two to five years. Then they tunnel to the surface, climb the tree, and emerge as adults through a split in the back of their larval skin.

Nymphs of the closely related periodical cicadas remain in the ground 13 or 17 years. Look for skin casings on tree trunks, then the five-eighths-inch hole in the earth from which the nymph emerged. Sometimes you'll find a three-inch-high mud "chimney."

Waltz of the Bluefish

There will come a morning in July when the wind falls and black shards, seemingly independent of mass, cleave the glassy surface of the Atlantic Ocean. They vanish and reappear mysteriously, then form daisy chains that may be 30 feet across. What you are watching are the tails of a toothy, voracious species whose scientific name, *Pomatomus saltatrix*, means "sheathed, leaping, cutting edge." But if you thought bluefish were always gluttonous, run a lure through the school and, more often than not, you'll have to cast again. For a few fleeting hours, these sleek predators are thinking about sex instead of food. It won't be long, however, before they are again charging about, lacerating anything in their path, sometimes including people.

You can locate feeding blues by the oil slicks created when they chop up baitfish. Even when wind or fog prevents you from seeing a slick, you can often smell it — a fresh, pleasant scent, vaguely reminiscent of sliced cucumbers.

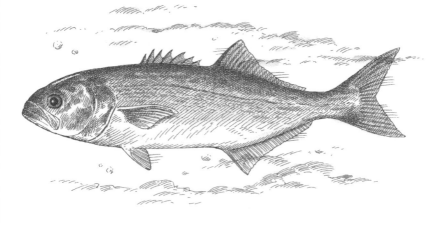

Tyrant of the Pond

Taxonomists call him **Tyrannus tyrannus,** a tyrant flycatcher. Take a seat beside a pond or marsh on a lazy summer's day, and you'll understand why. Before you see the eastern kingbird you may hear him — an electrical buzz from a bare branch with a good view:

"kip-kip-kipper-kipper," "dzee-dzee-dzee," and "dzeet." Eastern kingbirds summer almost everywhere in North America, though you'll have better luck finding them in the East.

In defense of its nest this pert, bigheaded little bird with the white tail band shrinks from nothing. It will stoop, falconlike, on crows, hawks, or eagles that stray into its airspace, pecking their heads and necks and sometimes riding on their backs for 100 yards. Toss your hat into the air and it may stoop on that, too. Eastern kingbirds have even been seen attacking airplanes.

Wrote ornithologist Ned Dearborn early in the twentieth century, "At times . . . the bird becomes a veritable fury, and dashes upward toward the clouds, crying fiercely, and ever and anon reaching a frenzied climax, when its cry is prolonged into a kind of shriek, and its flight a zigzag of blind rage. These exhibitions are frequently given in the teeth of the premonitory gust before a thunderstorm, as if in defiance of the very elements."

Quarter-Ounce Bug Bomb

Throughout most of the United States the quarter-ounce little brown bat dips and wheels through the summer twilight, netting insects in skin stretched between its hind legs and tail. At this time of year the female will return to her roost several times a night to nurse her pup, which she cradles in her soft wings.

While bats get rabies, they are no more prone to the disease than any other mammal, and if you don't plan on handling them or dunking them in your beer (as did one victim for reasons he took with him to the grave), it is safe to share your attic with any species. The ability of the little brown bat to consume 1,200 mosquito-size insects in an hour often makes it a welcome houseguest.

People who insist on sealing bats "out" of their attics frequently seal them in instead, thereby killing them and creating an odor problem that would otherwise never have existed. Sometimes you can attract bats to your yard by erecting bat roosting boxes. Hang them in an open, sunny area — not from a living tree. Boxes are offered on the website of Bat Conservation International (see Resources).

If reclamation of a subsurface mine is underway in your area, make sure bats aren't being buried alive. In Michigan, Bat Conservation International intervened in a scheduled mine reclamation that would have wiped out a million little and big brown bats — the continent's second largest hibernating colony.

While white-nose syndrome, an alien fungus disease, has drastically reduced little brown bat populations, there is recent evidence that they are building resistance.

Belated Breeders

In July and August, when other birds are already fledging their second broods, American goldfinches (known also as wild canaries) finally get around to nest building in most of their range. Capturing their personality, the great ornithologist Edward Howe Forbush wrote: "'Panoplied in jet and gold,' the merry, care-free Goldfinches in cheery companies flit in the summer sunshine."

But these birds have a better excuse than frivolity for late nesting. Midsummer brings two essentials to the lives of breeding goldfinches — ripe seeds for nourishment and ripe thistle silk for nest building. Hatchlings, only a few days old, have been found in October.

In eastern North America west to the southern Rockies, look for the male's breeding flight, characterized by deep dives with wings folded and upward sweeps with wings outstretched. During this display he utters his normal flight call — "Per-chick-o-ree." If the female calls when the male is circling over the nest, he will drop down to feed her.

Mini Tuna

Little tunny, a.k.a. false albacore and fat Alberts, patrol tropical and subtropical waters on both sides of the Atlantic. But when ocean temperatures peak in late summer, they stream north as far as Maine and Great Britain in shimmering, elliptical shoals that can cover two miles on the long axis. Most people, even experienced anglers, think they're bluefish or striped bass. Watch for the sickle tails and geysers of spray as these mini tunas swill bay anchovies and other baitfish. Often the school is attended by a cloud of screaming terns and gulls that dip and dive for leftovers. Few of these short-lived, fast-growing fish weigh more than 15 pounds, but when they take your fly, they'll have 50 yards of line off the reel before you can snatch your bruised knuckles from the spinning handle.

Fueling Hummers

July seems awfully early to start a fall migration, but now male rufous hummingbirds are setting out on the longest treks of any U.S. hummer. Females will follow soon. Instead of taking their spring route along the Pacific coast from Mexico to as far north as Alaska, they move south along the Rockies, sipping nectar from flowers throughout most of the West.

Both sexes will aggressively defend feeding areas even when satiated. Males face their opponents, so they've evolved bright scarlet-orange throat patches. But because females often warn away competition by fanning and waving their tails, they've evolved distinctive tail patterns. When flowers are scarce rufous hummers will drink sap from holes drilled in trees by sapsuckers; and they will come readily to sugar-water feeders.

Boil four parts water for 15 seconds, then add one part sugar. Let cool, and do not add coloring. If the sugar-water in the feeder turns opaque, change it and scrub the inside of the feeder. On a cold morning you may find a rufous hummer in such a state of torpor that you can pick it up. It will slowly revive in the heat of your hand, and you can refuel it by inserting its beak into an eyedropper of sugar water.

A Celestial Spectacle

Every summer a heavy shower is forecast between about July 23 and August 22. You'll get a better show if the sky is cloudless because it will be raining meteors. This is the Perseid meteor shower, when Earth slashes through the debris trail of the comet Swift-Tuttle. Only one other meteor shower — the Leonids in November — is as dazzling. The Perseids usually peak on the evening of August 12.

The meteors, moving at about 44 miles per second and usually no bigger than a pebble, will leave luminous trails of ionized atoms in the thermosphere 50 to 75 miles up. They will seem to emanate from the constellation Perseus. Lie on your back so that your gaze covers a wide area of the sky. You'll do better just before dawn when your patch of planet is rotating in the same direction as Earth's orbit. (This is why a driver sees more snowflakes strike the front windshield than the rear.) With luck and insomnia you'll see about one meteor per minute.

Wide Jaws

Save for dimpling mackerel and the tide trails of lobster-pot buoys, the summer sea is still. Suddenly a dorsal fin cleaves the surface, then another and another. Clearly they belong to sharks, huge sharks. You start noticing the diagnostic features of great whites — the tail lobes almost equal in length, the horizontal stabilizer keels on the caudal peduncle, the lighter-colored underside — and you can't get the famous line from *Jaws* out of your head: "We need a bigger boat!"

The cavernous, gaping mouth heading for you is at once startling and reassuring. Not even great whites can open that wide. These are basking sharks, the sole member of the family Cetorhinidae and the planet's second biggest fish after the whale shark. Basking sharks, which can weigh 8,000 pounds and approach 30 feet in length, patrol the world's temperate oceans, lazily filtering plankton through their gill rakers. Look closer and you'll see the physical characteristics of this species — tiny, vestigial teeth, long gill slits that almost encircle the head, and a snout reminiscent of an elephant seal.

In the nineteenth and twentieth centuries basking sharks were commercially plundered for their oil-rich livers, which account for a quarter of their body weight. Today little exploitation occurs outside China and Japan.

Scent of High Summer

Long after most plants have blossomed, sweet pepperbush fills the air with a fragrance that freezes the fleeting hours of August, drugs the droning bee, and transports aging wanderers of woods and water to a time when summer never ended and one's only commitments were to fish, frogs, and turtles. This leafy shrub, also known as summer sweet, grows best with full sunlight in wet soil from southern Maine to Florida and as far west as Texas. The tiny white flowers appear in clusters on upright spikes, which make fine air fresheners if your car smells of, say, wet dog.

A Sky Full of Goatsuckers

You may look up in late August to see a sky full of darting, dipping nighthawks massing for fall migration. Note the white crossbar under the long, sharp wings. The bird is not a hawk but a member of the "goatsucker" family. Like all goatsuckers the common nighthawk has a cavernous mouth that lets it clamp onto the teats of she goats under the cover of darkness, the better to suck them dry — or so claimed farmers of yore. Its name notwithstanding, this bird favors insects, not milk.

Unlike most other goatsuckers (whip-poor-wills and chuck-will's-widows, for example) it is abundant in town and country throughout most of North and Central America. This is because it has adapted to urban and suburban life, nesting on gravel-topped roofs and using its mouth to scoop up flying insects attracted to city lights. The stomach of one engorged nighthawk contained 2,175 flying ants.

Flowers You Can't Pick

To borrow Thoreau's description, a bladderwort stands out in a drab, frost-burnt bog like "a sluttish woman with a gaudy yellow bonnet" in a congregation of Puritans. Bladderworts, found throughout most of the nation and on every continent save Antarctica, usually have a pair of liplike yellow petals, and North American species often bloom well into November.

You can't pick a bladderwort because it has no roots and you'll lift the whole plant when you pull. Bladderworts float in water or wet moss, supported by green threadlike, bladder-equipped leaves. The species obtains nutrients by trapping and eating aquatic organisms such as water fleas and mosquito larvae. When a victim brushes one of the trigger hairs on a bladder, a trapdoor opens, sucking it in. Digestion, facilitated by enzymes and bacteria, takes between 15 minutes and two hours.

Lift a bladderwort and hold it to your ear. The faint popping you hear is caused by the bladders gulping air. According to some reports, it sounds like "Feed me."

Stranded in Summer

As summer wanes, larvae of tropical fish, many associated with coral reefs, drift north on the Gulf Stream, settling into tepid bays and estuaries along the eastern seaboard, where they metamorphose into miniature replicas of their parents. Offshore shelves are arranged in such a pattern that the south of Cape Cod seems to be the barrier.

Drag a fine-mesh net across the shallows, and you may find butterfly fish, angelfish, barracuda, triggerfish, snowy grouper, rock hind, blue runner, jack crevalle, orange-spotted filefish, coronet-fish, permit, mullet, and bigeye. For a few weeks these southerners thrive in ideal habitat, but they are stranded in the summer of an alien world. When the year's first nor'easters chill the North Atlantic, they all die.

Bloom of Sea Spray

The sky is unblemished cobalt, the air still and fragrant with the scent of tidal flats and sun-baked driftwood. So what are those curtains of blue-gray spray rolling across the Atlantic shore? They are the tiny flowers of a low, erect perennial called sea lavender or marsh rosemary. In late summer and autumn they brighten salt marshes and wet meadows from Labrador to Florida. Thick rootstocks contain a powerful astringent formerly used for treatment of dysentery, hemorrhage, and bad breath. Like other native plants of marine wetlands, sea lavender can be wiped out when humans, in vain efforts at storm-surge flood control, block tidal flows, thereby creating monocultures of invasive phragmites.

Beautify Your Yard

The bananas are black, the pears mushy, and melon rinds from your houseguests are piled around your sink. So what are you waiting for? Just toss it all onto the grass. That way you can attract some of North America's most colorful and ubiquitous butterflies — red-spotted purples, occurring in every state and active in the warmer months, especially now. Watch as they imbibe the fermented juices, opening and closing their wings in seeming delight. The upper and under sides are strikingly different — the former, iridescent black and purple fringed with tiny white spots; the latter (which gave rise to the insect's name), decorated with striking reddish brown and orange spots.

In northern states you may have noticed butterflies that are identical save for broad, white median bands on the upper sides of both wings. These "white admirals," as they're called, had been thought to be genetically distinct, but now most taxonomists believe they're just different forms of the same species. Where the two forms overlap there is hybridization. Hybridization also occurs with the closely related viceroy, which derives protection from predators by mimicking the color pattern of the toxic monarch. Employing the same strategy, the red-spotted purple mimics the toxic pipevine swallowtail.

While few butterflies are more beautiful than red-spotted purples, their cream and brown caterpillars look like, well, scat — specifically, bird droppings. By this mimicry they, too, derive protection from predators.

Little Fish of Big Country

Chestnut-flanked and flecked with scarlet spots centered in azure halos, the brook trout is gaudy in any season. But as spawning nears in September, the belly of the male turns sunrise-orange, and the ivory trim on the edges of his lower fins gets more vivid. Brook trout are little fish of big country, inhabiting forgotten, magic places where oxygen-charged springwater tumbles over mossy ledges and curls off through alder runs and boggy meadows.

They're not really trout but descendants of oceangoing char landlocked by ancient ice sheets. Before the species was widely transplanted in the West it was called the "eastern brook trout."

No perennial rill is too small for these glacial relics. Populations can miniaturize to fit the habitat, with adults no longer than your thumb. Walk along any high-country or north-country stream and you're apt to see them scoot. Or maybe when swamp maples blush and woodcock twitter through bare alders, you'll find them paired up, hovering over quartz gravel in water so clear you can't tell where it stops and the air begins.

Tasty Trees

Now, in the southeast quarter of our nation, large, straight-trunked trees are draped with thorny, cherry-shaped seed-balls hard enough to puncture tires. Scrape the tree's corky bark, and you'll smell the reason it is called sweet gum. Scrape harder, and you get tasty chewing gum.

Swirling to Sleep

A good month before bat renderings adorn school windows and shopping mall aisles, real bats drift southward, swirling around the entrances of their winter hibernacula — usually caves or abandoned mine shafts. Some species, such as the mothlike eastern pippistrelle (so small it can fit through a dime-size hole), roost or hibernate in caves and mines year-round. Others, such as the little brown bat, found throughout most of the nation except the Southeast, roost in hollow trees and buildings during warm months, entering caves and mines only to escape the desiccation and freezing temperatures of winter.

Male little brown bats arrive at the entrance first, attracting females with calls too high-pitched for human ears. After mating, females store sperm in their uteri through the winter. Ovulation and fertilization occur in early spring, birth in early summer.

Bats are in trouble worldwide. In North America an alien fungal disease, white-nose syndrome, has sent them into steep decline. And in temperate regions around the globe, human disruption of hibernacula is a major limiting factor. The expenditure of energy by wintering bats rousted by intruders can cause them to starve. The appearance of just one spelunker can destroy an entire colony.

Eastern Pippistrelle

Little Brown Bat

Salmon Recycling

From Point Hope, Alaska, to Monterey, California, coho salmon are in various stages of their spawning run. The species' threatened and endangered status south of the Columbia River tends to obscure the fact that it thrives throughout most of its natural range.

Fresh from the cold sea after 16 to 20 months of voracious feeding, cohos are chrome bright, with backs that are blue-green and richly spotted. You'll see them more easily after they spend a few days in fresh water, because they turn red. They become swimming gametes, with all surplus energy redirected to the testes or ovaries. Muscles decay; skin peels away; white patches of fungus bloom on head and back.

With rotting tail, the hen cuts a depression in gravel; attended by at least one male, she deposits her eggs. Then, as with all five species of North American Pacific salmon, the adults die, and their decomposing bodies fertilize sterile river tops, nourishing the ecosystems that sustain their young.

Rushing Fall

The August sun is bright and hot. With so many summer things left to do, the last thing you want to think about is winter — unless, that is, you're a purple martin. Uttering musical chirps and raspy twitters, these large, loud swallows hawk dragonflies and, as the day ends, swirl like coal smoke around trees, rising, settling, finally roosting. Within hours they'll strike out for Bolivia, Paraguay, and Brazil.

You're apt to encounter purple martins almost anywhere in the contiguous states. And while they're not as common as they were a century ago, they're recovering in some areas of the East thanks to multiunit "purple martin hotels" erected by bird lovers. The eastern subspecies has been conditioned to artificial nest sites for centuries, first by the Choctaw and Chickasaw people, who hung out gourds for them. Now it's almost entirely dependent on nest boxes.

Hotels with two dozen or fewer rooms work better than bigger ones. Rooms should be at least six inches on a side, and it's important to provide good ventilation and drainage. A coat of white paint will help cool nests by reflecting sunlight. Hotels should be placed in the open and mounted on high metal poles. To discourage house sparrows and starlings, plug entrance holes until martins show up.

How to Find Cows

When grass goes gold and the bright, still air is full of milkweed silk and cricket song, the daddy longlegs goes a-courting. Now sexually mature and fully grown, these gangly arachnids leave their summer haunts amid dead and living vegetation. Suddenly they seem to be everywhere, which is why farmers of yore called them "harvestmen."

Worldwide there are at least 7,000 species of daddy longlegs, all of which lack the spiders' fangs, poison, and silk glands. Where a spider has two distinct body parts, a daddy longlegs has one, and instead of having eight eyes like a spider, it has two, mounted on a small turret near the front of its body. A male spider must transfer its sperm to the female on the tip of an armlike appendage called a pedipalp. Daddy longlegs, on the other hand, can copulate. A daddy longlegs chews and swallows its prey instead of sucking out the body fluids, and it also consumes fruit and plants.

Its second pair of legs — the longest — is used more for sensory perception than locomotion. These are waved at whatever the creature happens to be investigating and always, say country folk, in the direction of cows.

Mini Beaver

As summer wanes, mountain beavers start weaning their young. If you live in the Northwest, you may glimpse them at dusk as they venture from their elaborate burrows for the night's foraging. But you don't have to restrict your search to mountains; and don't look for anything remotely resembling those paddle-tailed dam builders that abound in river systems across the continent. The mountain beaver, with no living family relative, is about the size, shape, and color of a muskrat. And like so many other burrowing rodents, it is richly bewhiskered and has small ears, eyes, and tail.

The most primitive of all rodents, it traces its ancestry to the early Tertiary Period, some 40 million years ago, when mammals had just started to assert themselves in global ecosystems. Mountain beavers construct elaborate tunnels with bathrooms, bedrooms, pantries (stocked with vegetation that they have allowed to dry on the surface), and as many as 30 exit/entrance holes. Droppings are stored and reingested once, making for more efficient metabolism of woody forage. Habitat in forested sites is frequently dominated by red alder, partly because the animals select for it by eating seedlings of such competing vegetation as conifers.

Free Riders

In mid-September vast "kettles" of broad-winged hawks spiral up on buoyant thermals that waft from the sunbaked earth. When these medium-size, short-tailed buteos get to the top of the thermal, they break away and glide to the next. In this fashion they can cover 250 miles a day without a wingbeat.

Broadwings also use updrafts created when northwesterly winds slam into mountains. Position yourself on a mountaintop reported to be a good hawk "lookout." You can see migrating broadwings almost anywhere in the United States, but in the East more than 1,000 may sweep over your head in 10 minutes. You'll see other species, too. If you can't get to a known lookout, don't despair. You can discover your own by checking out high, windy ridges.

Fragrance of Indian Summer

There is a pause between summer and fall, when nights are cool and full of cricket song, when swamp maples blush, and when limbs along the meadow's edge bend low with fruit. Among the first of these fruits to ripen are wild grapes — about 30 species throughout our nation, mostly native and often natural hybrids.

Wild grapes feed a host of wildlife, including bears, foxes, skunks, opossums, doves, grouse, quail, prairie chickens, wild turkeys, woodland thrushes, woodpeckers, cardinals, and at least 100 other songbirds. The fragrance of wild grapes carries so far and is so unmistakable that the best way to find them is with your nose. There are plenty for everybody, so don't hesitate to pick some; their tartness makes them perfect for jelly.

Save the green ones because they contain natural pectin; in fact, if you pick enough green grapes, you won't have to add pectin. Cover grapes with water, crush, boil 20 minutes. Let sit 10 hours. Strain the juice through cheesecloth. Four cups juice, four cups sugar, one box pectin (less depending on number of green grapes). Boil. Skim the foam. Pour into sterilized jars. Seal.

Summer's Scarlet Farewell

When streams run out of song and speed, and woodland ponds shrivel to mud-rimmed sumps, wetlands receive a new infusion of color. From New Brunswick to Florida and west to east Texas, the cardinal flower, one of the continent's most striking native perennials, is in full bloom. The five-petaled, scarlet blossoms are about two inches long and pollinated almost exclusively by hummingbirds.

Bittersweet is the first flash of cardinal flowers from a desiccated wetland, for as surely as blushing swamp maples, it means that summer is winding down.

Green Lynx's Orange Eggs

Lynxes are more abundant than you imagined. In fields, prairies, open woods, scrublands, yards, and gardens from Maryland to California and south to Florida and Mexico they're hunting down prey. The female needs a lot of it now because her eggs are forming. She's slightly more than a half inch long with spiny legs and a bright green body — North America's largest lynx spider, so named because of the way she stalks and pounces on insects and arachnids.

Soon she'll construct her egg sac, flattened on one side, rounded on the other, half an inch to slightly more than an inch in diameter, and filled with 50 to 600 orange eggs. By now her color may have changed to match her surroundings. Sitting on top of her egg sac or hanging from it on a strand of silk, she guards it aggressively, rushing at any intruder.

When the spiderlings hatch later in the fall she tears a hole in the sac for them. And she protects them for about 10 days until they lay out silk parachutes and float away on the autumn breeze. If you listen carefully you can hear their high, thin voices shouting "Goodbye" (at least according to E. B. White).

Fall

While not immune to spring-induced giddiness, members of the Williams family are far more afflicted with a previously undescribed malady called fall fever. We feel the first symptoms on those crisp mornings, just prior to the autumnal equinox, when morning glories open on the latticework along the south garden wall, when our lake falls silent save for the lapping of waves and the gabbling of northern ducks, when aspens and tamaracks go smoky gold, swamp maples blaze, and the azure sky is one shade richer than at any other time of year.

Fall brings the fragrance of woodsmoke and leaf smoke, the sweet-rotten scent of frost-killed ferns and deer-bitten apples, young grouse in the touch-me-nots, woodcocks fluttering mothlike into bare alder runs at dusk, wild geese barking as if from treetop level, yet so high they look like ribbons of crepe tacked to the corners of the crescent moon. As Joni Mitchell and our friend Tom Rush sing, they've got the "urge for going."

Migrations of geese and other waterfowl are noticed by most people, even those otherwise oblivious to the natural world. But the greatest migrations on Earth pass unseen by all but a few thousand Americans. They happen not with mammals on Old-World steppes or savannas or even with birds along busy flyways, but with sea creatures underwater along our West and East Coasts.

At the neck of the eastern funnel — the inshore rips off Montauk, New York — my friends and I are at hand to watch and participate. Bobbing in little boats, we jockey for position around "boils" of striped bass packed so tightly that our flies sometimes ride on their backs. Such boils happen nowhere else. Bluefish — that bite off our flies and, if we're careless, slash our fingers — encircle the stripers. Orbiting the bluefish are the shining mini tunas called false albacore, green backs cleaving the surface faster than anyone who hasn't caught one believes a fish can swim. Bay anchovies — "rainbait" — erupt in panicked sprays. Screaming terns and gulls pick them — along with sand eels, silversides, bunker, herring, and mullet — virtually from the maws of preda- tor fish. Volleys of gannets fall into the waves as if shot by medieval archers.

Sometimes when we squirt the ocean with our onboard hoses, "albies," as we affectionately call false albacore, show up expecting rainbait. Out beyond the albies lurk bigger tunas, mackerels, marlins, swordfish, carnivorous sharks, whale sharks, basking sharks, dorado, ocean sunfish, leatherback sea turtles, porpoises, whales. . . .

At home, though, we pay the most attention to birds. As so many familiar species leave our yard and meadow, our appreciation grows for those that stay. Particularly beloved are chickadees whose language we have studied and come to understand; bluebirds who, recently in the Northeast, have forgotten they're supposed to fly south and instead stay all winter, feasting on winterberries and, when they finish these, mealworms that I keep in the refrigerator in cloth bags and that give Donna the heebie-jeebies when they occasionally escape; the bossy Carolina wrens, loudest and smallest of our residents, who take over the yard and eat everything from suet to sunflower seeds and cracked corn; the handsome, jaunty cedar waxwings, who, with our bluebirds and winter robins, swill our winterberries; bluejays, more melodious than anyone who doesn't pay attention to them can imagine; screech owls, who whinny at us on frosty nights; and, of course, our crows, who amuse us in countless ways, such as by soaking all manner of offal, including French fries and roadkills, in our granite birdbath.

Sometimes on still nights we'll drive to the hickory grove beside Poler's Pond and park with the headlights on. It takes about 10 minutes for the southern flying squirrels — a.k.a. "fairydiddles" — to resume their nut gathering.

They'll glide down from the hill, frequently for 100 yards, swoop up onto a trunk, and chase each other up the shagbark. Or they'll parachute straight from the crowns, landing beside the car.

Once, after Beth and I had watched them for an hour, I sent her to bed, only to see her promptly reappear in the family room, claiming that a fairydiddle was perched on the curtain of her bedside window. I ordered her back to bed and told her it was just her imagination. But it wasn't. Flying squirrels don't fear humans because they almost never see them, and this one watched Beth calmly as she set out a dish of nuts, a hamster water bottle, and a metal exercise wheel. About three o'clock that morning I heard the wheel spinning for perhaps 30 minutes. At daybreak the nuts were gone. "Peanut," as Beth named the pet that had chosen her, stayed for three weeks, then left, apparently the same way he'd come in.

The earth is fat in fall, dripping milk and honey into the mouths of wild creatures and into the souls of humans, who will soon be entering their own form of hibernation in front of flickering fires and flickering screens. It seems that all the other seasons have been building up to this one. As nature writer Hal Borland put it: "It was for ripeness in and all around us that winter passed and spring and summer found us."

Golden Oldies

From Newfoundland south to Delaware and northwest to Alaska, the round, dancing leaves of the quaking aspen — our most widely distributed tree — glow neon yellow as they catch the rays of the low-arcing sun. Tree texts have it that quaking aspen is short-lived. "Old at 50," says one. Aspens, however, should be thought of not as trees but as root systems. The "trees" are really clones sent up by the main part of the organism. Inject a radioactive isotope into one clone, and it will show up in another 10 feet away. A single root system may underlie a whole hill and weigh 32 tons to the acre.

Aspen doesn't do well in dry habitats such as Yellowstone National Park, so why is there so much of it there? Botanist Roy Renkin thinks aspen may have gotten started in the park when the climate there was cold and wet — i.e., during the Ice Age. If so, aspens could be the oldest living things on Earth.

Blood of the Great Bear

In autumn, Ursa Major descends from northern skies to pad along hardwood canopies, leaving them bright as he fades into dawn. According to Iroquois lore, ancient hunters killed the Great Bear, and the carcass bled on maples, sumacs, dogwoods, sweetgum, blackgum, sassafras, and the like, staining them crimson. When the hunters cooked his flesh the dripping fat stained yellow the leaves of such trees as aspens, birches, hickories, elms, beeches, cottonwoods, and willows.

This explanation is no more fanciful than the currently popular notion that autumn leaves are tinted by freezing temperatures. Foliage is dulled, not colored, by Jack Frost. Reds are brightest when sunny days are followed by cool (but not freezing) nights. Under such conditions sun-made sugars are trapped in the leaves, where they form the red pigment anthocyanin.

Leaves that appear yellow in fall are no less so in spring and summer. It's just that the yellow pigments — carotenoids and xanthophylls — are masked by the green pigment chlorophyll, which breaks down with diminished sunlight. Find maple leaves that are still green and tape black paper over parts of them. Shielded from sunlight, these parts will turn yellow, while exposed parts turn red.

Explosive Jewels

In autumn roadsides and meadow edges from Newfoundland to Saskatchewan and Florida to Nebraska explode in color as the orange, slipper-shaped blossoms of spotted jewelweed unfurl. Soon thereafter the ripe seedpods literally explode when jostled by beast or wind, sending seeds flying in all directions — hence the plant's alternate name "touch-me-not." The azure seeds, which taste like butternuts, were eaten by various indigenous tribes, and they're relished by birds and small mammals. When white-footed mice hoard them they stain their bellies blue.

The name "jewelweed" derives from the water-repellent quality of the leaves that causes dew and rain to bead up and sparkle in the sun. If you're afflicted by poison ivy, poison oak, or athlete's foot, dramatic relief can often be had by crushing the stems and applying the sticky paste to affected areas.

At times jewelweed can be invasive in gardens, but in dismissing it as a "dreadful weed nuisance" the *New York Times* elicited the ire of biology professor Mary Leck of Rider University in Lawrenceville, New Jersey. After citing all the above attributes of this remarkable plant, she offered this: "On reflection, perhaps jewelweed is truly a potential deterrent to the gardener — it may offer too many distractions from gardening chores."

Autumn Reveille

You'll hear it one morning in the Mountain West, when the first frosts burn the purple sage and southbound waterfowl settle into creek bottoms. The low, clear note increases in volume to a scream, then fades to a series of short grunts. At the edge of a meadow or along a ridgeline, the bugler, maddened by hormones, stands with his head to the sky, neck swollen with blood, venting steam from his nostrils; churning the ground with his hooves; thrashing shrubs with his immense, back-swept antlers; spraying urine on his belly, hocks, and mane. During the rut, bull elk bugle to assert their dominance over their harems and to challenge rival bulls. The larger the bull, the deeper-pitched his bugle.

There used to be an eastern subspecies, but it was ushered into extinction by unregulated hunting. The last eastern elk in the Appalachians, and perhaps east of the Mississippi, was killed in 1867 in what is now Elk County, Pennsylvania.

Flight of the Flickers

Unless you're watching for their fall migration, northern flickers — North America's most abundant woodpeckers — will slip past you like Indian summer. In southern Canada and all our northern states, there are more flickers moving now than during the more intermittent spring migration, but they have long since shouted themselves out. No more do raucous flocks bob through the trees, calling excitedly. Instead they flow in steady, stately flight high over the brightening forest canopy, silent as the monarch butterflies that share their airspace.

Most will spend the winter in the southern United States, and some will find refuge by drilling their way into vacant buildings. Unlike other woodpeckers, flickers spend much time on the ground, foraging for insects, especially ants. One flicker's stomach contained about 5,000 ants, two others 3,000 each.

There are two subspecies, each named for the color of feathers on the bottom of wings and tail — yellow-shafted in the East and red-shafted in the West. On the Great Plains they meet and interbreed.

Riches to Rags

The fur of the ermine or short-tailed weasel was worn by kings — but only if procured in winter when white and punctuated by the black tail tip. "Royal ermine," it was called. But as cool weather creeps over Europe, Eurasia, and North America from tundra to latitudes as far south as central California and northern Virginia, ermine look more ragamuffin than "royal." Now they're splotched brown and white as winter pelage replaces that of summer.

A big male might weigh almost a pound and measure 18 inches, including its 5-inch tail. But what the species lacks

in size it makes up for in ferocity and fearlessness. It has even been seen to attack foxes, badgers, raptors, and domestic cats, all of which will prey on it, given the opportunity. Ermine are active mostly at night, so look for them early and late in the day in marshes, forest edges, wet and open woodlands, meadows, and hedgerows.

Dark Clouds on the Horizon

The day is windless and cloudless with a sky the shade of azure you see only in September. So why is there a shifting, swirling black cloud above that distant barrier island? Line it up in your spotting scope, and you'll discover it's several hundred thousand tree swallows, staging for migration to their winter habitat in the southern states. Other swallows have to push on to Central and South America because they depend entirely on insects. During the cold months, however, tree swallows can subsist largely on fruit — especially bayberries.

In addition to their flocking behavior, these highly social birds engage in an apparent game in which they drop a feather from considerable altitudes, then compete to see who can snatch it. The winner climbs and drops the feather again. Offspring from the previous year will assist parents in feeding hatchlings.

Tree swallows are doing better these days thanks to the great popularity of bluebird boxes into which European starlings — one of their major nesting competitors — cannot fit.

Puff the Magic Fungus

Puffballs, those fungi that appear throughout most of North America after autumn rains, on rich humus and over buried stumps, seem made for kids. The smoke that spews from the hole atop the dry, leathery husk when you tap it or step on it is spores from the already-dead fruit. So fine are these spores that they can drift to elevations of five miles and travel between continents. The giant puffball, which sometimes reaches four feet in diameter, may produce 7 trillion spores annually.

But the magic doesn't end here. Depending on which of the 270 species you encounter, a puffball may grow from the size of a golf ball to the size of a baseball in a single night. Moreover, the main part of the plant — the mycelium — lives underground and extends in all directions through the soil, sometimes creating a circle of puffballs above. A much older — and, some would argue, better — explanation has it that these circular growth patterns are set by the feet of dancing fairies; hence the popular name "fairy rings." Since this theory cannot be disproved, why hasten its extinction when you are afield with young companions?

Woolly Bear Wisdom

In our culture caterpillars are not much beloved. But there is one exception — the ubiquitous woolly bear, larva of the Isabella tiger moth. Who, while strolling in a crisp autumn afternoon most anywhere in our nation, has not stooped to rescue this portly ball of fur from the blacktop? Instantly, it curls up. Maybe you bounce it on your palm, feeling the bristles, before gently dropping it into roadside grass.

Woolly bears, which pupate in spring, are frequently encountered as they seek winter dens. Among caterpillars this is unusual behavior. Folklore has it that one may predict the severity of the coming season by measuring the brown (middle) band — the shorter the band, the colder the winter. Actually, the brown band may tell you something about the winter, but only the previous one. The more brown hairs, the older the caterpillar. A long winter delays hatching, resulting in a younger caterpillar and a thinner band.

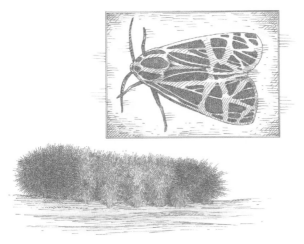

Polterguests

House mice — ship stowaways from Europe — infest human dwellings. Our cleaner natives — the ubiquitous white-footed mouse and the closely related deer mouse — visit. They arrive in camp by moonlight and starlight, entering like poltergeists through openings unseen and unknown when the first hoarfrost silvers understory leaves and the swamp maples match the embers in your woodstove. East of the Rockies, save in Florida, you may see at least one of these creatures in the light of the dying fire, flowing over floor and hearth, pausing to preen its luxuriant fur and impossibly long tail, fixing you with huge, obsidian eyes.

White-footed mice tend to be woodland dwellers, but you're likely to encounter deer mice in most any terrain. Neither species hibernates, so they need your place more than you do. They might shred some paper and poop on the counters; otherwise, they're easy guests. In spring they always leave.

Eyes South

Throughout most of the United States, buckeye butterflies are wafting south, sometimes in concentrations that rival the famous fall migration of monarchs. Look for these midsize butterflies in clearings and along meadow edges as they fuel up on the nectar of asters and other late-blooming wildflowers. Often they'll be perched on a protruding branch or the ground. If another insect passes close by, they're likely to give chase, then return to their posts. The six striking, multicolored eye spots — two on each hindwing and one on each forewing — are thought to frighten insectivorous birds.

Adults live for only about ten days, but butterflies of the last brood can overwinter if they make it to southern states and countries. In spring buckeyes breed themselves back to their summer habitat, rolling north in waves of successive generations.

Prickly Passion

In early fall throughout most of North America from the Arctic Ocean to northern Mexico — on forestland, grassland, tundra, and desert — porcupines are breeding, or thinking about it.

One might suppose that sex would be an extremely delicate affair for these squint-eyed, yellow-toothed pincushions. But it is not noteworthy in that regard. What is noteworthy is that it is frequently initiated by the female through high-pitched vocalizations, vaginal secretions, and urine markings. The male follows her, serenading with voluminous humming and grunting.

One might also suppose that the birth of the single "porcupette" (about 210 days after copulation) would be an extremely painful affair. But during delivery its quills are soft, hardening an hour later.

The word *porcupine* derives from the Old French *porc-espin*, meaning thorny hog. A porcupine carries some 30,000 barbed, easily detachable quills, but it is stingy with them, preferring to retreat before surrendering any to an attacker. If a porcupine bristles and chatters at you, it is wise not to advance. Pass the word to your dog.

Clown-Faced Hoarders

In the Southwest and far West, acorn woodpeckers are tapping acorns — and occasionally walnuts, almonds, and pecans — into hundreds of holes they've excavated in dead trees and even telephone poles. A single tree or pole may contain 50,000 nuts for late-winter sustenance, and if a nut dries and shrinks, a bird will carefully move it to a better-fitting hole. It takes several generations to dig enough holes for the group to store the acorns needed for winter, so storage trees are family heirlooms.

Even the most clinical researcher can't stifle a smile upon seeing these red-capped, white-eyed, clown-faced birds storing or defending their hoard. They do everything — even raise young — in family groups. Potential thieves such as squirrels and jays are raucously set upon by mothers, fathers, sisters, brothers, uncles, aunts, and cousins, all diving and shouting "ya-cup, ya-cup, ya-cup."

Under Milkweed

Common milkweed has been used to treat dropsy, dyspepsia, asthma, and scrofula. But perhaps it is most effective as a tonic for receding youth and a preservative of the bright, quiet hours of Indian summer. In dry, forgotten fields from Canada south to Kansas, Tennessee, and the Georgia highlands, tufts of silk protrude from the sun-split pods like stuffing from puppy-ripped pillows. When golden popple leaves tremble in the September breeze and the sky goes cobalt, the seed-bearing parachutes of ripe milkweed seem to launch best on the breath of children. Whole hillsides have been planted this way.

Remember where the parachutes land, because next spring the tender shoots will provide excellent table fare, similar to asparagus. Boil for 15 minutes, changing the water frequently with fresh boiling water. (Cold water would fix the plant's bitter juice, which can be mildly toxic to humans.)

Buck Rubs

Who has been stripping bark from the two-inch-thick sapling at the edge of your lawn? Certainly not a rabbit, because the fresh wound extends to a height of three feet. At this time of year, probably not a porcupine. Even if you live in crowded suburbia, there's a good chance the vandal is a male white-tailed deer, our nation's most abundant ungulate, whose numbers are thought to be higher today than when English boot prints first defiled Virginia sand.

Maybe you'll see him against the blush of dawn, pushing the sapling and shaking his head, his glistening antlers protruding through shredded velvet — the fuzzy, blood-rich tissue that has nourished them since they sprouted last spring. Bucks may rub more to leave their scent than to unsheathe their antlers. But soon the last shred of dried velvet will tear away, and the battles of autumn will begin.

Stay-at-Home Dads

Wilson's phalaropes are moving from American and Canadian prairie country to saline lakes, where they'll molt and put on fat for their migration to winter habitat in South America. This species differs from the other two members of the genus in that it is larger, breeds exclusively in North America, is limited to the New World, and spends no time at sea. But like its cousins, it has reversed sex roles. The female acquires colorful breeding plumage, defends territory, and attracts her mate vocally and with displays that include neck stretches and feather puffing. After the male scrapes out a nest site and lines it with grass, the female lays about four eggs and departs, leaving incubation and rearing to her mate.

Something like half the population of Wilson's phalarope, estimated to 1.5 million, congregates on Utah's Great Salt Lake before pressing south. Watch for them as they swim rapidly in tight circles, creating whirlpools that bring up invertebrate prey such as brine shrimp. Or you may find them facing breaking waves as they let the wind do the work for them.

Wilson's phalaropes seem to be compensating, at least in part, for loss of wetland breeding habitat on the prairies by expanding their range. They're now being seen in southeastern Alaska, New Mexico, and even Massachusetts.

Charlotte's Children

One morning in early fall, your lawn may be draped with a silver fabric bright enough to mimic a pond's surface but so fine it seems to have no mass. Chaucer called the phenomenon one of the unsolved mysteries of the universe. Subsequent investigators attributed it to evaporated dew. It took a pig to pin it down: "The baby spiders felt the warm updraft. One spider climbed to the top of the fence. Then it did something that came as a great surprise to Wilbur. The spider stood on its head, pointed its spinnerets in the air, and let loose a cloud of fine silk. The silk formed a balloon. As Wilbur watched, the spider let go of the fence and rose into the air."

That passage, from E. B. White's *Charlotte's Web*, remains one of the best descriptions of how many juvenile North American spiders disperse. Darwin observed silk-riding spiderlings when the *Beagle* was 60 miles from land. In May 1884, 10 months after one of the most powerful volcanic explosions in history sterilized the island of Krakatoa, the first scientist to set foot on the site found only one life-form: a spiderling. Census traps mounted on airplanes have caught spiderlings at 15,000 feet. Occasionally, they'll ascend to the jet stream and cross the Atlantic.

Deep Purple Fall

As the growing season slows and the coolness of Indian summer settles from cobalt skies, pokeweed seems to leap out from meadow, fencerow, and roadside. Throughout the East and in the far West north to Oregon this fast-growing perennial herb is suddenly about as tall as you, and its once-drab berry clusters have gone from green to white to spectacular purple. Birds — especially robins, towhees, mockingbirds, mourning doves, catbirds, and bluebirds — feast on this fruit, spreading seeds in their droppings and decorating your car, sidewalk, and outside furniture with purple stains. (Rain and sun removes them better than soap and water.)

Concoctions from sundry parts of the plant are said to soothe sore nipples of nursing mothers and ease symptoms of autoimmune diseases, tonsillitis, mumps, glandular fever, sprains, and cancer. Red pigment from the berries has been used as dye and ink. And in much of the range, especially the South, young shoots and leaves, collected earlier in the year when they're less toxic, are boiled with two water changes and eaten like spinach. Soon pokeweed may die back to the roots, and poke enthusiasts will dig and dice them, then cultivate a new supply of tender shoots in their cellars.

Poisonous Hope

"Don't worry, there are no poisonous snakes in this state."
Unless you live in Maine, Rhode Island, or Alaska, that persistent reassurance is incorrect — at least the second half of it. Don't worry — in fact, rejoice, but from Florida to Massachusetts and west to southern mid-America, you've at least got copperheads.

You are unlikely to encounter these shy, docile, beautiful pit vipers unless you go looking for them, and early fall is the time. Now they congregate at the entrances of their dens on rocky hillsides with southern exposures. But watch where you step, because copperheads respond to danger by going motionless. When the nights turn cold, they settle in for the winter, often sharing their quarters with timber rattlers and black rat snakes.

It is well that the outdoors still contains an element of danger, however slight. Creatures like copperheads impart hope to those who care about wildland, reminding us that we have not entirely sterilized it — that in a few places, forces other than humanity remain in charge.

Helicopter Migration

Not all dragonflies die with summer. In late September one of our largest and fastest, the green darner, masses for migration. Watch for large flights over sunny fields throughout North America.

Dragonflies have four independently powered wings that enable them to hover, fly backward, and attain speeds of up to 30 mph. Sometimes they fly in tandem, the male grasping the head of the female with his tail. He does this to discourage competing males who, otherwise, would extract his sperm from a storage pouch inside the female and replace it with their own. A few dragonflies have 2½-foot wingspans — the ones engraved in 200-million-year-old fossils.

No one knows where or how far green darners migrate because there isn't a practical way of marking them. But Mike May of Rutgers University thinks they fly to Florida, the Gulf Coast, and, perhaps, to Mexico. He bases this theory on large groups seen all along the route, voracious feeding, and reports of mass movements associated with a single cold front, particularly along the eastern seaboard.

Flue Fliers

At twilight a black funnel cloud forms in a windless and otherwise unblemished sky. But instead of sucking up the building over which it hovers, the building sucks it down until only a few wisps, swirling like candle soot, fade into the gathering darkness. Swifts, massing for fall migration, have dropped into their night roost in an unused chimney. In the Northwest the species is Vaux's swift; east of the Rockies it's

the chimney swift. Both are often the victims of chimney sweeps or of fires kindled by people who don't know the birds are there.

Related to hummingbirds, swifts have cigar-shaped bodies; long, narrow wings; and feet so puny they can only cling to vertical surfaces. Wings quivering, large mouths agape, they orbit parks, fields, and backyards, describing wild loops, chipping loudly. During the day they live in the air, eating, bathing, copulating, gathering nesting materials, and possibly sleeping on the wing.

If you have swifts roosting or nesting in your chimney, close the damper to keep the birds from falling into the fireplace. Despite the oft-told wives' tale, nests pose no fire hazard, and removing them is a violation of the Migratory Bird Treaty Act. If you don't have a chimney and want swifts, you can set up a swift tower. For plans, see page 238.

Colorful Collaborators

Lichens, which flourish in some of the harshest regions on Earth and may live for as long as 1,000 years, are now at their most colorful. This is because of the abundance of water in early spring. A particularly striking species is the British soldier, named for its scarlet-topped stalks. Another is the yellow map lichen, resembling smashed miniature bathroom tiles, perhaps from the dollhouse vandalized by "two bad mice" in Beatrix Potter's children's classic of that title. It was Potter, a keen observer and illustrator of nature, who was among the first to figure out that lichen isn't a plant but two cooperating plants. The fungus provides support and protection for the alga, which reciprocates with carbohydrates.

Two theories have been advanced to explain those mysterious rings of lichen on rocks and logs: plants growing outward at the same rate while the older ones in the center die; and circle-dancing fairies.

Researchers now use lichens to map air quality because they die easily when subjected to pollutants such as sulfur dioxide. In polluted regions of northern Siberia, for instance, the number of lichens has dropped from 50 to 3.

The effectiveness of lichens as medicine has improved steadily since the Middle Ages, when their use was determined by appearance. For example, lungwort was prescribed for TB, yellow lichens for jaundice, dog lichen for rabies. Today they seem to work better when used in antibiotic creams.

Sound and Fury

In fall the noisy, sassy Douglas squirrel — more aptly called the chickaree — provides comic relief in the big, solemn evergreen forests of the Pacific Northwest. At this time of year he is out and about, collecting pine cones and stashing them in hollow logs, where they'll keep for years. Interrupt him at his work, and he'll give you an earful. He is, in the words of nature writer Anita Nygaard, "A leaping, bounding, chattering gambol of energy and fury." The ear tufts he grows in the northern winter; the dark-red, turpentine-scented coat; and, especially, his personality call to mind his Old-World cousin — Beatrix Potter's impertinent Squirrel Nutkin. Look for the piles of pine cone scales he leaves on stumps.

Finer Art

Autumn shows more subtle beauty after wild winds waste the golds and scarlets of October. On the first really cold night, when woodsmoke rises straight into a cloudless sky and the shadow part of the moon is lit by starlight and earthshine, hoarfrost will adorn grass and facing hardwood leaves. At first light it will dazzle you.

Hoarfrost, white from air bubbles, and with etchings that resemble feathers, trees, ferns, or flowers, is an analogue of dew. But it is not frozen dew. Its intricate, interlocking crystals grow when water vapor turns directly to ice, skipping the liquid stage. There are two basic types of hoarfrost — the early variety you encounter now, and that which occurs more in midwinter and includes renderings on frozen streams and ponds.

Skinny Skunk

Not all skunks are portly, pokey waddlers — the image projected by the ubiquitous striped skunk. From British Columbia to Idaho and Wyoming south to Texas and Mexico, a smaller, quicker, longer-legged species is entering its breeding season. Unlike the striped skunk and the eastern spotted skunk (only recently recognized as a separate species), the western spotted skunk mates in autumn, and the fertilized eggs float around the uterus until early spring, when they attach to the uterine walls and develop anew.

There is virtually nothing edible that a western spotted skunk won't eat. Watch one hunt or forage, and you'll be reminded more of a weasel or house cat than what you've come to think of as a skunk. Unlike the striped skunk, the western spotted skunk is an excellent tree climber and an accomplished mouser.

It's almost worth the risk of getting sprayed to watch this stand-up comic perform its threat-display routine. First, it will stamp its front paws. If you stand your ground, it will then stiffen and strut like a politician on stump. Finally it will stand on its front paws, waving its butt and hind legs in the air.

If you're more than 15 feet away, you may or may not be okay. Some experienced observers find the odor of the spotted skunk somewhat "sweeter" than that of the striped skunk. But no one is saying "sweet" is good.

High-Country Jousting

Bighorns, among the world's largest wild sheep, can weigh more than 300 pounds and carry 20 pounds of horns. So when rams butt heads in late autumn, the percussions carry for miles through the thin mountain air of the American West. Competing for control of a band of ewes, two jousters, steadied by rubberlike cushions on the bottom of their hooves, will clash at speeds of about 20 miles per hour from as far away as 30 feet, and they may keep at it for 20 hours. Rarely do these contests result in serious injury, because the shock is absorbed by double-layered skulls.

Bighorn populations have been drastically reduced by parasites and pathogens associated with domestic sheep, by habitat destruction caused by livestock grazing, and, in the days before modern wildlife management, by unregulated market hunting. Now, with the help of sportsmen, they are being restored to much of their former range.

Planter of the Western Woods

The Clark's nutcracker is a big part of the spirit of the western evergreen forest. Sometimes he is brash and loud, dipping out of the canopy with a nasal "kra-a-a" as the day's first light slashes through the spires of conifers. Sometimes he is sedate and stately, sculling crowlike over the alpine forest, sun flashing on the white patches on his black wings and tail. Around your camp he may be a beggar and a thief. On otherwise still winter days, he raucously patrols south-facing slopes, recovering the pine seeds he tapped into the earth with his long, sharp bill during late summer and fall. There may be only 4 or 5 seeds per cache, but his total store may contain as many as 33,000, and he can tote 95 at a time in a special pouch under his tongue.

Recent experiments have demonstrated that nutcrackers use forest features to help them remember the locations of their seed caches. If a feature — a log, for instance — is moved 10 feet north, a bird will look for its seeds 10 feet north of where they really are. Because Clark's nutcrackers never recover all their seeds, they help plant the forest that sustains them.

Attractive Stench

The aroma of **Phallus ravenelii,** now wafting from woods, lawns, and gardens of eastern North America, is one of the more pleasing aspects of early autumn — if you're a fly. Flies glut themselves on the slimy, gray coating of this mushroom and then, thanks to its laxative properties, deposit the spores. Humans, less enthusiastic, have difficulty deciding if the scent resembles fresh feces or old carrion. For this reason they call the generally similar species of this wide-ranging genus "stinkhorn." In both the New and Old World you can find stinkhorns merely with your nose, and when you see one you will understand the reason for the generic name because, down to the last anatomically correct detail, it resembles a phallus.

Charles Darwin's daughter, Etty, sought to cleanse Victorian England of these allegedly obscene fungi, as Etty's niece, Gwen Raverat, recalls in her book *Period Piece*: "Armed with a basket and a pointed stick, and wearing special hunting cloak and gloves, she would sniff her way round the wood, pausing here and there, her nostrils twitching . . . then at last, with a deadly pounce, she would fall upon her victim, and poke his putrid carcass into her basket. At the end of the day's sport, the catch was brought back and burnt in the deepest secrecy on the drawing-room fire, with the door locked; because of the morals of the maids."

Hovering around stinkhorns, like the flies that spread them, are superstitions. Stinkhorns were said to be attached to the sexually aroused undead zombie community reclining in the earth. Mature fruits were consumed as aphrodisiacs and rubbed on bulls to make them strong.

Stinkhorns grow from white or pink, gelatin-covered "eggs" that are relished as delicacies in some parts of the world. Dig one up, and if you can resist eating it, keep it in a warm, moist place. In barely more than a day it will develop into a mushroom.

Bully for Bullwinkle

From the Rockies east, moose, Earth's largest deer, are filtering south, recolonizing traditional range as the species gradually rebounds from the unregulated hunting of the nineteenth century. In New England, moose are even recolonizing suburbia; recently they've been encountered in southern Connecticut. If you have seen heart-shaped tracks too big to be white-tailed deer, listen for the vocalizations of rutting bulls — moans, whines, and a series of grunts that, while not loud, are so deep that they carry long distances.

Moose, which are at the southern fringe of their range in the contiguous United States and therefore don't need the thermal cover that deer require, are benefiting from clearcutting. The practice encourages nutritious leafy growth and, at least in the north woods, it destroys deer habitat. This, too, is beneficial for moose, because deer are commonly infested with a brainworm that they carry with apparent impunity. But when the same brainworm infests moose, it blinds, maddens, and eventually kills them.

South of Canada and Alaska, winter is almost a lark for moose. In fact, these animals frequently choose to spend the winter on north-facing slopes. Thirty-inch snowfields that can cause white-tailed deer to founder and die barely impede moose: highly unsaturated fat in their feet remains in a liquid state, protecting them from ice and snow — an adaptation also found in wolves.

Despite the moose-hunting tip offered by waggish critics — "Take 10 steps back and shoot" — the resource is generally well managed. But a recent limiting factor, apparently the result of global warming, is the profusion of deer ticks. In much of New England deer ticks are now so abundant that they are killing moose, especially young ones.

Silk Purses

When autumn dies so do the beautiful black-and-yellow orb weavers whose dew-spangled webs stretched across garden paths and meadow grass just about everywhere in the contiguous 48 states. But during winter young garden spiders hatch in sacks that may contain as many as 1,400 eggs. They molt inside, then emerge in spring, crawling off or flying away on silk parachutes thrown to the wind. Look for the pear-shaped, inch-long, paperlike sacks hanging from tall weed and grass stems, especially in locations where you've seen webs.

Pretty Poison

In an ironic twist of nature, the milkweed's toxins, which apparently evolved to protect it from insects, attract monarch butterflies. Their caterpillars, which feed almost exclusively on milkweed, ingest sufficient poison to protect them from birds even after they have become adults. A bird that eats a monarch and does not vomit may die. Another butterfly species, the smaller viceroy, mimics the monarch's striking orange, black-veined pattern as a means of protection.

In autumn, monarchs migrate, sometimes covering 2,400 miles. Unless you watch carefully, you'll miss the show, because they travel in a strong, gliding flight very different from the erratic, bobbing courses of other species.

Lie on your back in a field on a still October afternoon and you'll see them at all elevations — a steady procession of color from Canada and the United States to the fir-clad mountains of central Mexico or the pine groves of coastal California. None of these migrants was alive in the spring. And virtually none of the wintering adults make it back to Canada. Instead, they breed their way home, as successive generations leapfrog along the north-moving wave of sprouting milkweed.

You can attract the nectar-drinking adults to your property by allowing part of your yard to revert to such tall wildflowers as asters, goldenrod, and thistle. Encourage monarchs to breed by collecting ripe milkweed pods, blowing the parachutes, and studiously ignoring neighbors who say you're weird.

Alien Beauty

The invasive, exotic plants we call "weeds" should be controlled where possible. But you need only detest what they do to the rest of our biota and the stupidity and carelessness that displaced them from their native soil. It's okay to appreciate weeds as individuals.

Consider the common teasel of Eurasia, so named because it was long used to card, or "tease," wool. Teasel, apparently introduced to the New World in the eighteenth century, is now extant in the eastern half of the United States and spreading via our interstate highway system.

By late fall the gaudy, purple flower heads, which were worn by medieval knights, have withered, and their egg-shaped skeletons, with their intricate geometric spines and markings, stand against the gales of November. Unless crushed by snow or cut for dried-flower arrangements, they will keep standing all winter.

The Gall of Goldenrod

If you are a fisherman seeking live bait (a scarce commodity in chilly weather) or just a curious naturalist, get thee to a goldenrod field, especially in the northern half of the country. Bring kids. Look on the stems for galls, bulbous growths that are the plant's reaction to insect attack.

Goldenrod hosts about 50 species of gall makers, but if you find spherical galls about three-quarters of an inch in diameter, chances are they were made by the larvae of the goldenrod gall fly. Before it pupates in spring, a larva will bore an exit hole to the edge. Split the gall with a jackknife, and you'll see the larva, hard and immobile but protected by its own antifreeze. Bring it inside your house, and in a few minutes it will start to wriggle.

If you would like to watch the fly emerge in late spring, leave the gall outside through February, since the larva can't complete its life cycle without an extended period of cold.

Flat on Their Sides

When the first nor'easters of fall send weakfish, bluefish, tunas, striped bass, marlin, and other Atlantic predator fish streaming south along the continental shelf, winter flounder — a.k.a. mud dabs, blackbacks, lemon sole — begin their own migration, easing in from deep water to bays and estuaries from Labrador to Georgia. Here, protected from frigid water by antifreeze in their blood, they'll spawn in midwinter, their eggs sinking, unlike the buoyant eggs of most other marine fish.

Winter flounder rest on the bottom, venturing higher in the water column less frequently than more piscivorous members of the order. Lying on their white blind sides and gazing up with bulging eyes that, during fryhood, have migrated to the right side of their heads, they are perfectly camouflaged against (or in) mud, sand, and weed. The first — and only — thing you are likely to see is their eyes. Winter flounder lack the large, toothy maws of halibut and fluke, and their thick lips are permanently puckered, as if waiting for your kiss.

Few fish are better eating, and now is the time to pursue them. Use small, long-shanked hooks. Sea worms work best, but garden worms are nearly as effective and easier to come by. Paint your sinkers red.

Frogs of Fall

Most other frogs stop talking in autumn, but the green frog, which abounds from the East Coast as far west as the lake states and east Texas, can't quite shut up. Males are far quieter now than in spring and summer when they were more aggressively defending territories and trying to call in females, but they insist on getting the last word. They'll sit for hours, leaving the long, cool evenings to the crickets and katydids, then announce their presence to the world with a loud banjo twang.

The tadpoles frequently hibernate before transformation, so if you see one at this time of year, chances are it's a juvenile green frog; another good possibility is the slightly larger, slightly less abundant bullfrog. The one sure way to distinguish between adults of these strikingly similar species is by the two ridge lines that run down each side of the green frog's back. Like bullfrogs, green frogs are voracious predators, glutting themselves on insects, fish, crayfish, other frogs, and even small snakes, mammals, and birds.

You can feed green frogs by loosely attaching a piece of fish or meat to a string and dancing it in front of them. Watch as they stuff it into their mouths with both "hands."

Beshrewed

What's that quick, beady-eyed little rodent with the sharp face, popping up and giving you the once-over? It's a shrew — not a rodent at all, but an insectivore. Shrews, the smallest and among the most common mammals in North America, abound throughout most of our nation, but rarely do we see them, because they spend so much time in tunnels, made in the earth or snow by moles and voles. Late fall, before snow provides them with insulation, is the best time to see most of the continent's 20 species; that's when they must hunt even more frantically than usual to maintain their metabolisms.

You'll see dead shrews more frequently than live ones, for two main reasons: One, a predator has killed them, then been repulsed by their strong musk (obviously an inefficient defense mechanism but probably useful in marking territories); or two, they have suffered "cold starvation" by losing heat faster than they could generate it. The smaller the object, the larger the surface area in relation to volume; so shrews chill out faster than other mammals.

One species, the short-tailed shrew, is venomous. With its red teeth it delivers nerve poison that can instantly paralyze an animal as much as 20 times its size. The poison, however, wears off quickly, so the short-tailed shrew has to eat its meal with great haste. Fortunately for the species, this is never a problem.

Crow Time

When the yet-snowless woods are silent save for the rustle of southbound wings and brown leaves clutched by oak fingers, one tends to notice crows. Penciled on gray sky, strung out high and low, they scull purposefully to and from roosts at dusk and dawn. Most will be American crows, our biggest crow, which are seen almost everywhere in the nation.

Mark their comings and goings and you may discover their winter roost. One important clue: The ground beneath will be littered with regurgitated pellets of compacted fur, hide, and bone.

The main criterion for a roost is shelter. It may be located in dense conifers, in thick hardwoods, or even in low brush or lakeside reeds. Where winters are mild, a roosting congregation may be enormous; 200,000 birds once occupied just 20 acres in Arlington National Cemetery.

When our economy was more agricultural, crows were regarded as the personification of evil. Not only did they steal our food, but they insulted us in the process by perching on the arms of scarecrows. As recently as the 1930s we'd dynamite their winter roosts, killing thousands in a single detonation. Crows are better appreciated these days, in part because we compete less with them. But even when we persecuted crows, we admired them for qualities we saw in ourselves.

American crows are aptly named. They belong in and to our land. They are loud, resourceful, durable, and adaptable. They live in wilderness and megalopolis, prospering with or without us. They are part of smoke-scented twilights and crisp, otherwise silent mornings, part of what we were, are, and hope to be. And whatever we leave it with or without, they are part of our future.

Silver Threads among the Gold

From southern Canada to Mexico, fall webworms are spinning silver threads among the gold, red, and green hardwood leaves. The webs resemble the earlier work of eastern tent caterpillars, but you won't find them in the forks of branches. Look for them instead where the branch tips are etched against the bright September sky, then think like Aldo Leopold, who wrote, "If the land mechanism as a whole is good, then every part is good."

Fall webworms are the communal larvae of a diminutive white moth that overwinters on the ground as a pupa, emerges in spring and summer, and lays eggs on the leaves of at least 120 species of deciduous trees. The trees are not seriously injured, because they evolved with fall webworms, because the growing season is essentially over, and because these native insects come with their own set of natural checks and balances. Yellow warblers, for instance, feed on the caterpillars, and at least two species of hornets carry them off to their young. Poke around in a web and you may find hollow caterpillars, eaten from the inside out by larval wasps.

Fish of Steel

Did you really see that flash deep in the silted, swollen flow? If you're not sure, move upstream to the first falls. Never will you be quite ready for the silver fish that hurtles into the cold, wet air and hangs across black conifers or gray sky. It is a steelhead — the big, powerful, migratory strain of rainbow trout fresh from the North Pacific, or the Great Lakes, where it has been introduced.

Toughest of all Pacific salmonids, the steelhead endures in dammed, dewatered rivers where our five West Coast salmon species are flickering out. And unlike Pacific salmon (with the exception of a few landlocked cherry salmon in Japan), steelhead don't always die after spawning. Frequently they mend and return to sea. Cut off from salt water by summer drought, they can survive in fresh water for a year, eating

almost nothing. A few will make five spawning runs during their lifetimes and attain weights approaching 50 pounds.

One threat to self-sustaining steelhead populations is hatcheries, which take eggs early to fill available space, thereby selecting against fish that run later in the year and for ones that do well in crowded, shadeless conditions (in short, selecting for everything wild trout are not).

Cattail Comforter

When the wild, discordant barking of geese turns your head toward Polaris, and the north wind sends cattail fluff swirling across the frozen marsh, it seems, as Joni Mitchell and Tom Rush sing, that "all that stays is dying." It's an illusion. Pick apart some cattail seed heads (common in most of the country), tossing the tiny parachutes soap-bubble-style to the breeze, but keep your eyes on the cigar-shaped seed head. Where the fluff is still held together by silk you'll find yellow, brown-striped worms about a quarter inch long — the half-grown larvae of the cattail moth. The superb insulation of their winter homes allows the larvae to postpone pupation till late spring.

The Witching Flower

As the last flowers fade from eastern woodlands, one shrub salutes the passing season with a final burst of color. As late as Halloween and sometimes on into November, the yellow blooms of witch hazel shine through its bare branches like shavings from a cake of yellow soap. As the plant flowers, nutlike fruits from the previous season's blooms shrink and, with loud reports, shoot seeds as far as 50 feet.

Witch hazel likely derives its name from the Y-shaped "witching rods" fashioned from its branches by which a gifted few supposedly can locate subterranean water and metal. The Onondaga tribe of New York taught settlers how to make liniment and salve by boiling the leaves, twigs, and bark.

Crazy Flights

Ruffed grouse, which abide in all the Canadian provinces and the north country or high country of 36 U.S. states, are the most widely distributed native gamebirds on the continent. For all but a few hours of their lives, they are secretive and retiring, haunting brushy, forgotten places near stone walls and ancient cellar holes, bursting out of ripe touch-me-nots and grape tangles at the first, distant crunch of boot or paw. But on some unknown autumnal signal — folklore says it's the full moon — broods disperse in "crazy flights," striking out on all compass points, buzzing into places where none of their tribe, save themselves, would be found dead.

The young birds fly straight and fast, stopping for nothing. Look for them in such places as the rug in front of your picture window, amid the broken glass. One of the unpardonable sins for any outdoors person is to let a dead grouse go to waste. If you want to be completely legal about it, get a hunting license (a good investment for conservation anyway) and pick up crazy-flight victims only during the hunting season. Sauté the breast fillets with onions and mushrooms, then simmer everything in sherry and condensed mushroom soup.

Fairydiddles

Flying squirrels — a.k.a. "fairydiddles" — are probably more abundant than grays or reds, but you wouldn't know it because they're abroad only by dark. On still autumn evenings you can hear them tapping nuts into the forks of branches with their incisors, a sound once attributed to elfin cobblers. Take a seat in a hickory or oak grove or bait a feeding station with sunflower seeds, bacon grease, and peanut butter. Red light is nearby invisible to flying squirrels, so red plastic over your flashlight helps. In the East you'll most likely encounter the southern flying squirrel; in the West the slightly larger and less suburban northern.

These, our smallest squirrels, materialize as if by magic, parachuting straight to the forest floor or gliding 100 yards to another tree. Flying squirrels will hunch up and chart their course with rapid head movements, then leap, unfurling the flight cape by extending wrists and hind legs. They exhibit almost no fear of humans, often allowing themselves to be scratched and stroked.

It's hard not to wax anthropomorphic about these woodland sprites. They embrace while mating, the male throwing his cape over the female like an Austrian baron. They literally kiss members of their denning group. Strangers, on the other hand, are slapped in the face with the soles of the hind feet. They stamp when angry. In the midst of nut gathering, they will pause to bat a nut around. Or they'll chase each other up tree trunks and sail off through the night, chirping and twittering — as if in laughter at those who do not believe in fairydiddles simply because they never see them.

Beautiful Debris

When Earth intersects the orbit of the comet Tempel-Tuttle in mid-November, debris enters our thermosphere, vaporizing 50 to 75 miles up and leaving luminous trails of ionized atoms that seem to radiate from the constellation Leo the Lion. This annual event is called the Leonid meteor shower. But once every 33.2 years, Tempel-Tuttle swings through the inner solar system, dousing us with a huge load of junk. When this happens, the shower becomes a "storm," and if conditions are right, as many as 100 meteors are visible per second.

One account of the storm of 1833 reads as follows: "A tempest of falling stars broke over the earth. . . . From the Gulf of Mexico to Halifax, until daylight with some difficulty put an end to the display, the sky was scored in every direction with shining tracks and illuminated with majestic fireballs. At Boston the frequency of meteors was estimated to be about half that of flakes of snow in an average snowstorm."

The word "meteor" derives from the Middle English *metheour*, meaning "atmospheric phenomenon." That's what meteors were thought to be until 1833, but so prolific were they during that year's storm that observers noticed they issued from Leo, even as it rose into the southern sky. This proved that meteors were from outer space.

Fall Signs of Spring

With spring and nesting season half a year away, why are the ducks tearing up the marsh with elaborate courtship displays? It's a good question to which no one without webbed feet has a definite answer. By November or December most North American male ducks have replaced their dull eclipse garb with brilliant breeding plumage and are exhibiting bizarre posturing and weird vocalizations. Each species has its own displays, and all are worth watching.

Take the ubiquitous mallard. Two or more males will mill about with heads drawn in, shaking their tails and bills, sometimes stretching their necks and raising their breasts. Then, with bills pointed down, they will raise the backs of their necks, whistle, and toss up a spray of water. A hen may respond by rapidly swimming among her suitors, head outstretched and just grazing the water. Invariably this behavior elicits a burst of new displays from the drakes.

When a bonded pair is approached by a strange drake, the hen will utter a tremulous "quegegegegegege," scull closely behind her mate, and flick her bill to one side or the other. At other times both sexes will face each other and bob their heads rhythmically or mock preen, raising a wing and fanning the feathers to expose the bright blue speculum.

Meet Your Skinks

Now, when they are seeking winter dens in logs, mammal burrows, woodpiles, and stonewalls, is the best time to meet neighbors you may not have known you had. If you live east of the Great Plains and outside northern New England, your state probably hosts five-lined skinks. Some five-lined skinks indeed have five lines — from neck to mid-tail. But others, particularly older ones, do not. The head of the adult male is redder than the female's. When a male sees another five-lined skink, he charges with his mouth wide open; if the stranger turns out to be a rival male, a fight ensues.

Juveniles have bright blue tails, presumably to decoy natural enemies away from vital body parts. When a predator or person grabs the tail, it detaches, then wiggles seductively. Sphincter muscles in the stump close off the caudal artery, thereby preventing excessive blood loss. The lizard then grows a new tail, but one with different scales and more subdued coloration.

Keystone Fish

With the line storms of late autumn and early winter,
Atlantic menhaden — herringlike fish that spawn at sea —
move in colossal schools out of Northeast bays and estuaries, setting a course for their offshore wintering grounds
south of Cape Hatteras, North Carolina. On still days,
watch for what looks like rain squalls sweeping across the
ocean. If you are in a boat or standing on a dock or a bridge,
you may see silver, oval fish, 4 to 15 inches long, streaming
by with their mouths open and gills flared as they strain out
phytoplankton with their gill rakers. Often a school will be
attended below by crashing, boiling striped bass and bluefish, and above by screaming, diving gulls and terns — all
swilling protein for their own southbound migrations.

Sometimes the bluefish push menhaden onto beaches,
where they pile up in windrows miles long and up to three
feet high. Tuna, seals, porpoises, and sharks follow the orgy,
consuming the menhaden as well as the bass and the blues.

But by far the most efficient predators of menhaden are humans, who catch them in purse seines, landing 250,000 metric tons in some years. Most menhaden are rendered into animal feed and additives to plasticizers, resins, lipstick, shortenings, and margarine.

Always the menhaden defend against the slaughter with a fecundity that defies human imagination; and while there can be sharp population swings, they appear to result only from natural causes.

Lilliputian Forests

Imagine Earth a quarter-billion years ago — before dinosaurs, before flowering plants, when our planet was cloaked in towering forests of primitive, spore-producing trees. Today we burn them as coal. But as with so many ancient life-forms, they did not disappear; instead, they miniaturized.

There's no better time to walk through these relict Carboniferous forests than November, when their evergreen foliage imparts a sense of warmth and wonder to the otherwise bleak landscape of the temperate United States. But watch where you step, because the canopy doesn't rise above your boot tops. These tiny "trees" are called clubmosses, but they are more closely related to ferns than to true mosses. Some of their names are richly descriptive — wolf's paw, for example, and Robin Hood's hatband, forks and knives, tree branched, princess pine (a.k.a. ground cedar).

The use of club-mosses in Christmas wreaths has reduced their abundance to the point that picking them is now illegal in some states. A spore, less efficient than a seed, can take 7 years to reach the gametophyte stage; then the gametophyte can take an additional 10 to produce a mature plant — good reason to let club-mosses keep decorating the yuletide woods.

Snow Bunnies

As the days dwindle down, the fur of the snowshoe hare goes white; but unlike the pelage of other mammals — including, alas, our own — it will get brown again in spring. If a hare goes white before the snow falls, it's in big trouble because in bare hardwoods or black conifers it stands out like phosphorus in a night sea. The "snowshoe" part of its name derives from large, splayed hind feet that allow it to travel easily over snow.

Throughout its range from Alaska, across most of Canada and our northern states, and down the spines of the Rockies and Alleghenies, few prey species are more abundant or subject to wilder population swings. In good hare years predators such as owls, foxes, fishers, and lynx thrive. But as hares proliferate they deplete their bark-and-twig food supplies, triggering a population crash that soon extends to their major predators. Snowshoe hares provide more evidence that what we all learned in biology class is wrong and that, for the most part, it's prey that controls predators.

Don't Stand under Mistletoe

If you stand under wild American mistletoe — which grows in California and from New Jersey and Indiana to Florida and Texas — you may get something less welcome than a kiss. This is because the white berries, ripe in November, are relished by birds. The plant's seeds pass through avian digestive tracts, germinate on the bark of trees, and send roots into sap-conducting tissues. But most species of mistletoe are only partial parasites, because their evergreen leaves contain chlorophyll, which enables them to manufacture their own food once they have purloined water and minerals.

Ancient Europeans reasoned that because mistletoe bears fruit in the dead of winter, it must provide shelter for woodland spirits; hence its traditional use in rituals for fertility, health, peace, safety, and good luck.

Acknowledgments

Whatever success these essays have had or will have is attributable in no small way to the editors and fact-checkers with whom I've been blessed. I thank them all for their good work, good humor, patience, and, above all, their friendship. Special thanks to Connie Isbell, whom I have watched grow from a promising kid barely out of her teens to a brilliant, seasoned editor, who has been with me for every word of every essay, who thinks of the topics, who does a great deal of the research, and who was so essential to the column that she kept editing and researching it after she left *Audubon* to be an equally successful mom. I wouldn't — and probably couldn't — have done it without her.

Thanks to Roger Cohn for conceiving the idea of this column. Roger, the professional's professional, so demanding of excellence that he always gets more out of his writers than even they thought they had. I wish he were still at *Audubon* to share the fun of this. Thanks to David Seideman for his support and encouragement, his fearlessness, and his firm hand on the tiller of *Audubon* during perpetually foul weather. And thanks to Jerry Goodbody for his insightful fixes, his endless patience with my endless word dickering, for squeezing space in order to spare my words, and, especially, for the incredible hours he put in, doing the work of three people on one salary. On countless occasions I've called him at the office at nine P.M. or later, assuming he'd still be there. Mostly, I've been right. Thanks to Lisa Gosselin for believing in "Earth Almanac," expanding it, high-profiling it, and conceiving the new and better name.

Being a fact-checker is like being a defenseman in hockey. When things go right you get little of the credit, and when they go wrong you get most of the blame. Sydney Horton deserves a plaque in the Fact Checker's Hall of Fame. She's a natural, assuming that everything is wrong until she or I can prove otherwise. I cannot begin to count the times she has saved me from disaster and major embarrassment. If Sydney were a vegetable gardener, she would find the last tomato. Helping me greatly with fact-checking, as well as editing, have been Mary-Powel Thomas, Carolyn Shea, Yi Shun Lai, Chris Chang, Bob Frenay, Ingrid Eisenstadter, Gretel Schueller, Joshua Malbin, Keith Kloor, Matt Woods, Carol Capobianco, Tracie Matthews, Naomi Harris, and Abby Wheeler. When a subject has feathers, the people I call are Kenn Kaufman, *Audubon*'s (and everyone else's, for that matter) last word on birds, and my birding tutors and neighbors, Sue Finnegan and Mark Blazis.

Working tirelessly and successfully to make "Earth Almanac" attractive and readable and to acquire the most beautiful and dramatic photos available were *Audubon*'s art director Kevin Fisher, photo editor Kim Hubbard, and associate art director Isabel DeSousa.

Three people not associated with *Audubon* deserve special mention: Donna Williams, my favorite and toughest editor and the only one I ever married or even dated; my former colleague at the Massachusetts Division of Fisheries and Wildlife, Jim Cardoza — an encyclopedia for information on wildlife behavior; and Gail Howe (now Gail

Trenholm), a professional naturalist whose brain and library I ransack before each column, almost as a conditioned reflex — like clearing my desk and flexing my fingers.

There are editors, professors, and mentors living and dead who, while not directly involved in this copy, have contributed to it by making me a better writer. They are Mike Robbins, my erstwhile editor at *Audubon*; Les Line; Matt Miller; Greg Thomas; Joe Healy; Gary Soucie; Roxanna Sayre; Silvio Calabi; Jim Butler; Paul Guernsey; Charles Matthews; Mike Frome; John Voelker; Ted Densmore; Olin Ingham; Roger Duncan; Davenport Plummer; Mark Benbow; and Alfred Chapman.

TED WILLIAMS

Resources and References

Plans for building a "swift tower" can be found at
https://tpwd.texas.gov/publications/nonpwdpubs/media/
dwa_chimney_swift_information_2005.pdf

Bat houses are offered by Bat Conservation International, at
www.batcon.org

Poems Cited in Text

"All About Fireflies" by David McCord, in *The Star in the Pail*
(Little, Brown & Co., 1925)

"The Black Vulture" by George Sterling, in *The Little Book of
Modern Verse* (Houghton Mifflin, 1917)

"Blueberries" by Robert Frost, in *North of Boston* (Henry Holt,
1915)

"No shivering frond that shuns the blast . . ." by Willard Nelson
Clute, in *Our Ferns in Their Haunts* (Frederick A. Stokes
Company, 1901)

The Song of Hiawatha by Henry Wadsworth Longfellow
(Ticknor and Fields, 1855)

"A Wonderful Bird Is the Pelican" by Dixon Lanier Merritt
(publisher unknown, 1910)

Index